UNIONS AND LEARNING IN A GLOBAL ECONOMY

International and Comparative Perspectives

Unions and Learning in a Global Economy

International and Comparative Perspectives

BRUCE SPENCER, EDITOR
ATHABASCA UNIVERSITY

THOMPSON EDUCATIONAL PUBLISHING, INC.
TORONTO

Information on how to obtain copies of this book may be obtained from:

Web site: www.thompsonbooks.com
E-mail: publisher@thompsonbooks.com
Telephone: (416) 766-2763
Fax: (416) 766-0398

National Library of Canada Cataloguing in Publication Data

Main entry under title:

  Unions and learning in a global economy : international and comparative perspectives
Includes bibliographical references and index.

ISBN 1-55077-128-0
1. Labour unions and education. I. Spencer, Bruce
HD6483.U54 2002   331.8   C2002-900237-0

Copy Editing: Naomi Frankel

Every reasonable effort has been made to acquire permission for copyrighted materials used in this book and to acknowledge such permissions accurately. Any errors or omissions called to the publisher's attention will be corrected in future printings.

We acknowledge the support of the Government of Canada through the Book Publishing Industry Development Program for our publishing activities.

Printed in Canada.
  2 3 4 5   06

Table of Contents

UNIT III:
BUILDING THE UNION

UNIT IV:
CURRENT CHALLENGES

UNIT V:
REFLECTIONS ON THE FUTURE

About the Authors

- **GERALDINE CASTLETON** is Research Fellow in the Centre for Literacy and Language Education Research at Griffith University, Brisbane, Australia. Her research and publications include a focus on issues of equity and social justice, particularly for adults with limited literacy skills, in workplaces. She is also currently President of the Australian Council for Adult Literacy.

- **LINDA COOPER** has been involved in South African trade union education since the mid-1970s, first as a literacy worker, then as researcher and educator, and more recently as trainer of trade union educators. She lectures in the Centre for Higher Education Development at the University of Cape Town, and is currently doing doctoral research on aspects of learning within the labour movement. She is an education advisor to the national trade union education institute, Ditsela.

- **LYNN FEEKIN** has been involved in labour education for 25 years. She became active in the labour movement when she helped to organize her workplace for the Machinists Union. From 1976-1984 Lynn was part of the Labor Center staff at the University of Iowa, serving as its director from 1980-84. She joined the faculty of the Labor Education and Research Center, University of Oregon in 1994. In 1997 she had the opportunity to teach several extension classes for Australian unionists through the labour studies program at University of Adelaide in South Australia.

- **KEITH FORRESTER** works in the Continuing Education Department at the University of Leeds, England and is responsible for the learning, development and research work undertaken with trade unions in Britain and elsewhere. Current projects with trade unions include developing work and learning initiatives, supporting workplace learning representatives and piloting a "global labour" program. Keith has published widely on work, learning and labour education issues including the book *Workplace Learning: Perspectives on Education, Training and Work.*

- **NAOMI FRANKEL** has facilitated at the Prairie School for Union Women, and she has a son who for 51 weeks of the year waits impatiently for the beginning of the week-long Summer Camp for Kids run by the Saskatchewan Federation of Labour. She is an active member of the American Federation of Musicians and the Canadian Union of Public Employees. She coordinates education and training for a workforce of 4000 at the University of Saskatchewan.

- **GUNILLA HÄRNSTEN** is a pioneer in developing research circles as a link between universities and trade unions in Sweden. She has carried through several research circles with Swedish unions particularly the Swedish Municipal Workers Union and their different members, like female cooks and cleaners with whom she has developed feminist participatory research. She is associate professor in education at the Stockholm Institute of Teacher Education and has published books on socialist teacher organizations and on research circles.

- **CHRIS HOLLAND** is a co-founder and Associate Director of the national Workplace Basic Skills Network (Lancaster University). Chris is now an Associate Consultant, working from NZ. She has worked with key agencies (including the TUC, Trade Union Studies departments, and individual unions), and in Europe, the Republic of Ireland and New Zealand to improve professional development for teachers in the workplace. She is author of *Literacy and the New Work Order* (NIACE: 1998), Chris has written several recent papers on union interventions in workplace basic skills provision in the UK.

- **LARS HOLMSTRAND** has been engaged in developing the co-operation between Uppsala University and the unions in Middle Sweden since 1984, working with research circles and joint research program based on multidisciplinary research methods. He is associate professor of education at Uppsala, teaches union education courses and writes about research circles.

- **FRANCE LAURENDEAU** is director of the Collège FTQ- Fonds and is responsible for the overall coordination and planning of its future. She has worked for more than a decade on the FTQ research staff during which time she prepared many union policy statements, briefs and working papers. During a break in her union work she held research positions at the Université du Québec à Montréal.

- **FERNANDO AUGUSTO MOREIRA LOPES** is a Mechanical Engineer at the GERDAU S/A Iron Works. He is CNM-CUT Training Secretary (National Confederation of Metalworkers of the Unified Central Labour Congress, Brazil) and National Coordinator of the *Programa Integrar*.

- **D'ARCY MARTIN** has more than two decades of experience as a union educator in English-speaking Canada. This has included coordinating the Canadian education departments for the Steelworkers, the Communications Workers (and their successor the Communications, Energy and Paperworkers Union) and (in a job share with his partner Barb Thomas) the Service Employees International Union. He is currently coordinator of the

Centre for the Study of Education and Work at OISE/ University of Toronto. He is author of *Thinking Union: Activism and Education in Canada's Labour Movement.*

- **DOUG MILLER** currently works as a researcher on Multinationals for the International Textile Garment and Leather Workers Federation. Prior to this secondment from the University of Northumbria at Newcastle upon Tyne, UK, he worked extensively in training and research on European Works Councils for European Industry Federations, the Trades Union Congress (UK), the Dutch (FNV) and the German Trades Union Confederations (DGB) as well as several national trade unions.

- **MICHAEL NEWMAN** has worked as an adult educator for over thirty years in the community, union and university fields. In the 1980s he was a national trainer with the Australian Trade Union Training Authority. During the 1990s he was a Senior Lecturer in Adult Education at the University of Technology, Sydney. He remains an associate of the Faculty of Education at UTS. He has published a number of books including *The Third Contract: Theory and Practice in Trade Union Training; Defining the Enemy: Adult Education in Social Action* and *Maeler's Regard: Images of Adult Learning.*

- **TOM NESBIT**, a former official with the British Transport & General Worker's Union, has worked as a labour educator in Britain, Sweden, the USA, and Canada. He is the founding director of the Centre for Labour Studies at Simon Fraser University in Vancouver, British Columbia. His current research interests include union involvement with workplace literacy programs, education for union officials and staff, and a project to develop research skills amongst literacy practitioners.

- **BRUCE SPENCER** taught union education courses in the UK for 18 years before moving to Canada in 1990. He is a professor in the Centre for Work and Community Studies, Athabasca University (Alberta, Canada) and has written widely on labour and adult education issues. His most recent books include *The Purposes of Adult Education: A Guide for Students* and (co editor) *Learning for Life: Canadian Readings in Adult Education* both published by Thompson Educational Press in 1998.

- **JOHN STIRLING** is principal lecturer in industrial relations at the University of Northumbria in Newcastle upon Tyne. He has been involved in trade union education programs for over 20 years and has worked with the TUC in England, the European Trade Union College and the Commonwealth TUC as well as individual trade unions. He has published widely on the development of European Works Councils and the renewal of trade unions in the UK and Europe. He is joint editor (with Jeff Bridgford) of *Trade Union Education in Europe* (ETUCO, 2000).

- **JEFFERY TAYLOR** is professor and coordinator of labour studies in the Centre for Work and Community Studies at Athabasca University (Alberta, Canada). His most recent book is *Union Learning: Canadian Labour Education in the Twentieth Century* (Toronto: Thompson Educational Publishing, 2001) and he is currently investigating the relationship between workers and online learning.

- **MARCUS WIDENOR** began his career in the labour movement as an organizer for the International Ladies' Garment Workers' Union in Alabama. From 1979 until 1984 he worked at the University of Minnesota's Labor Education Service. He is currently an Associate Professor at the Labor Education and Research Center at the University of Oregon. In 1993 and 2000 he visited Australia to do research for studies of comparative US/Australian labour relations.

- **KENT WONG** is the director of the UCLA Center for Labor Research and Education, where he teaches labour and ethnic studies. Previously he was staff attorney for the Service Employees International Union #660 in Los Angeles. He served as founding president of the Asian Pacific American Labor Alliance, AFL-CIO, and is currently the president of United Association for Labor Education, representing union and university labour educators. Kent is the author of *Voices for Justice: Asian Pacific American Organizers and the New Labor Movement*, and co-author of *Voices from the Front Lines: Organizing Immigrant Workers in Los Angeles*.

- **RITA KWOK HOI YEE** is a founder of the Hong Kong Social Workers General Union. She has worked for two decades as an advisor and educator with unions like the Hong Kong Telecommunications Union, and was chair of the Hong Kong Trade Union Education Centre, affiliated with the Hong Kong Confederation of Trade Unions. She currently teaches at the School of Social Work in the Hong Kong Baptist University, and is preparing a book on the impact of economic changes on workers' rights in China.

Preface

Unions remain the most important and popular form of worker (or working class) organization in most liberal democracies. Labour education (education by and for unions) attracts more participants than any other form of non-vocational adult education in these countries and is one of the most important forms of adult education available to working people. But it is most often under-reported and ignored in discussions about adult learning, labour relations or generally in discussions about the role of unions in society.

Labour unions are regarded as "old" social movements, but as we look back on the past millennium, they have to be considered as a relatively recent social organization. If we set aside early forms of workers associations, "modern" labour or trade unions, with significant membership, probably did not emerge until the 1840s: they are approximately 160 years old. Workers' education in different forms predates modern labour unions, but a substantial offering of "independent working class education" can only realistically be dated back to the turn of the century (Simon, 1990). Labour education (education with the central purpose of supporting the union organizationally) is no more than 100 years old and it could probably be argued that the main characteristic of labour or union education – representative training – began no earlier than the 1920s. Of course, labour education draws from earlier forms of workers' education and could simply be treated as part of a continuum rather than a separate entity. For an illustration of this point as it applies to Canada, see Taylor (2001); for the US see London et al. (1990); and for the UK see Simon (1990). The point of this historic note is not to enter into, or attempt to settle, such a debate but rather to register the fact that no matter how it is defined, labour education is a relatively new project.

We should also note that neo-conservative and "post-industrial" commentators often predict the demise of labour unions but, in fact, unions remain stubbornly present within most liberal democracies. Union membership and union influence may have declined across the spectrum (except in Scandinavia) but it has not vanished. In some cases unions are making a comeback. For example, in Aotearoa/New Zealand a steep decline in the late 1980s and early 1990s, due largely to individualized employment contracts, is being reversed alongside a change in employment law. Organization, representation, negotiation, lobbying, strikes and other forms of union activity still occur worldwide. Labour education also persists and in some ways has been expanded, with, for example, a renewed emphasis on general membership education and on education for union organizing. Labour education has also begun to challenge new management techniques, issues of globalization, and workplace learning (usually interpreted as educating employees to be more valuable human resources). It has responded to calls for international workers' solidarity, to educational challenges posed by widespread computer use and the Internet, and to calls for marrying job preservation to environmental protection. There has also been some "rediscovery" of the role of traditional workers' education within labour education provision leading to a renewed focus on political economy and social analysis.

In many ways, therefore, this is an ideal time to produce a book of international and comparative readings on labour education, one that will reflect on what unions are doing and what they need to be considering, a book that discusses how labour education can contribute to a democratic and liberatory future for working people in the 21st century. Although the emphasis is on the developed English-speaking world, contributors come from eight countries (Australia, Brazil, Canada, China, South Africa, Sweden, UK, and the USA with one chapter drawing on a study of 15 European Economic Area countries; and another chapter from French-speaking Quebec) and span all populated continents. The labour education reported on in this book reflects the various political realities of the countries represented and enhance our understanding of how these political realities affect working people. The authors are leading labour and adult educators with union and labour relations backgrounds. They are authors of numerous studies of labour and adult education and of labour relations and labour studies books, articles, papers and reports.

This book of readings will be of interest to labour, popular and adult educators; union officials and members; college and university students and to those working in the field of labour/industrial relations and applied economics, no matter what sector or context they work in. It is very important for students of adult education, community development, workplace learning and labour relations to understand the contribution and centrality of labour education. It should be a key text in adult education and labour relations courses, particularly in English-speaking countries.

Book's origins

The motivation for the book came from an international meeting of labour educators attending an adult education conference in London (UK) in 1997. At that time I coordinated a special sub-group of labour educators and researchers to discuss issues of common concern. Mike Law (University of Waikato,

Aotearoa/New Zealand) suggested that an international labour education text was needed to advance our understanding of labour education issues worldwide. In Spring 2000, another international adult education conference was held in Vancouver (Canada) and again I organized a special labour education pre-conference. It was clear that an international text – but with a focus on English-speaking countries for practical reasons – was still needed. A book on international and comparative perspectives on labour education has never existed prior to this text. This book provides context, discusses issues and examples of provision, relates economic and labour relations challenges and trends, and reports on new initiatives, programming and courses. It also provides direction for labour education into the next century.

REFERENCES

- London, S., Tarr, E. & Wilson, J. (Eds.). (1990). *The re-education of the American working class.* New York: Greenwood.

- Simon, B. (Ed.). (1990). *The search for enlightenment: The working class and adult education in the twentieth century.* London: Lawrence and Wishart.

- Taylor, J. (2001). *Union learning: Canadian labour education in the twentieth century.* Toronto: Thompson Educational Publishing.

Abbreviations

ACTU	Australian Council of Trade Unions
AFL/CIO	American Federation of Labor - Congress of Industrial Organizations (US)
ALP	Australian Labour Party
AMWU	Australian Manufacturing Workers' Union
ANC	African National Congress
ANTA	Australian National Training Agency
APALA	Asian Pacific Labor Alliance (US)
AQF	Australian Qualifications Framework
BSA	Basic Skills Agency (UK)
CAW	Canadian Autoworkers
CBC	Canadian Broadcasting Corporation
CGIL	General Italian Union Confederation
CISL	Confederation of Italian Unions
CLC	Canadian Labour Congress
CNM	National Confederation of Metalworkers (Brazil)
COSATU	Congress of South African Trade Unions
CUPE	Canadian Union of Public Employees
CUPW	Canadian Union of Postal Workers
CUT	Unified Central Labour Union (Brazil)
CWJ	Campaign for Workers' Justice (APALA,US)
CWU	Communications Workers Union (UK)
DfEE	Department of Education and Employment (UK)
DGB	German Union Confederation
Ditsela	Development Institute for Training, Support and Education for Labour (SA)
EEA	European Economic Area
EC	European Community
ECU	European Currency Unit
EIF	European Industry Federations
ETUI	European Trade Union Institute

ETUC	European Trade Union College
EWC	European Works Council
Fedusa	Federation of Trade Unions of South Africa
FNV	Dutch Union Confederation
FTO	Full-Time Officer
FTQ	Fédération des travailleurs et travailleuses du Québec (Quebec Union Confederation, Canada)
HRM	Human resource management
IG Metall	German Industrial Metalworkers Union
ISO 9000	International Organization for Standardization
LCC	Labour College of Canada
LDSS	Joint Sustained Development Laboratories (Brazil)
LO (Swedish)	Swedish Confederation of Trade Unions
LO (Danish)	Danish Confederation of Trade Unions
LSO	Labour service organization (SA)
MNC	Multi-national corporation
NACTU	National Council of Trade Unions (SA)
NGO	Non-governmental organization
NQF	National Qualifications Framework (SA)
OI	Organizing Institute (US)
OW	Organising Works (AUS)
PEL	Paid educational leave
PID	Integration Program for the Unemployed (Brazil)
PSUW	Prairie School for Union Women (Canada)
R2L	Return to Learn (UNISON, UK)
SAK	Finnish Union Confederation
SEIU	Service Employees International Union (North America)
SFL	Saskatchewan Federation of Labour (Canada)
SWOP	Sociology of Work Unity, University of Witwatersand (SA)
TCO	Swedish Confederation of Professional Employees
TGWU	Transport and General Workers Union (UK)
TUC	Trade Union Congress (UK)
TUTA	Trade Union Training Authority (Australia)
UCLA	University of California in Los Angeles
UNISON	The Public Service Union (UK)
WELL	Workplace Language and Literacy (Australia)

1
Labour Education: An Introduction

BRUCE SPENCER

Labour education refers to education and training offered by labour unions (trade unions) to their members and representatives. The extent to which this education is provided directly by unions or by another agency or educational institution for unions varies from country to country and union to union. A main purpose of labour education[1] is to prepare and train union lay members to play an active role in the union. Another purpose is to educate activists and members about union policy, about changes in the union environment such as new management techniques, or about changes in labour law. Labour education is also used to develop union consciousness, to build common goals and to share organizing and campaigning experience. Unions have a small full-time staff and therefore rely on what is essentially voluntary activity of their members to be effective at work and in society; the labour education program is thus a major contributor to building an effective volunteer force.

Most labour union members learn about the union while on the job (what is often referred to as informal or incidental learning). They probably will learn more and become most active during negotiations, grievances and disputes, but they also learn from union publications and communications, from attending meetings, conferences and conventions, and from the union's educational programs. Although labour education only caters to a small number of members in any one year it is "social," as opposed to personal, education. It is designed to benefit a larger number of members because the course participants are expected to share the learning they have gained with other union members. Labour education has a social purpose – to promote and develop the union presence and purposes so as to advance the union collectively. Labour education can be described as essentially non-vocational, non-formal adult education with its origins rooted in the traditions of workers' education, the seeds of which are more than a century old and pre-date modern unions.

Core labour education

Most of the labour education courses provided by unions are *tools* courses (for example, shop steward training, grievance handling, health and safety

---

[1] The term "union education" can be used interchangeably with "labour education" in this chapter. "Union education" is sometimes reserved for courses run directly by unions as opposed to labour education courses run for unions (whether or not they are directly sponsored by unions) by other providers.

representative courses). The next largest category is *issues* courses (for example, sexual harassment, racism, or new human resource management strategies), which often seek to link workplace and societal issues. A third group of courses can be labelled *labour studies*, and they seek to examine the union context (for example, labour history, economics and politics).

Tools courses directly prepare members for active roles in the union, to become representatives of the union; tools courses are targeted at existing or potential union activists. They are provided directly by the unions, by labour federations or by union centrals (such as the Canadian Labour Congress [CLC], the UK Trade Union Congress [TUC], and the Swedish Confederation of Trade Unions [LO]). Tools courses are also provided for unions by educational institutions (for example by many of the labour studies centres across the US) by educational institutions collaboratively with the central bodies or individual unions (for example with colleges, universities and the Workers' Educational Association collaborating with the TUC in Britain). They may also be provided by specialized institutions such as the now defunct Australian Trade Union Training Authority (TUTA) or South Africa's Development Institute for the Training, Support and Education of Labour (Ditsela).

Many unions layer their courses, with introductory, intermediate and advanced courses and programs. Advanced courses are generally available to those who have completed introductory courses. Some of the introductory *tools* courses lead on to *issue* courses (sometimes referred to as "awareness" courses), which are specifically targeted at raising awareness and union action around the issues discussed. In some cases there will not be a strict demarcation between *tools* and *issues* courses nor a requirement to undertake one before the other, but the differentiation between types (and therefore the aims and purposes) of labour education can be useful for analytical purposes.

The union movement also provides more extensive and demanding educational opportunities such as the Harvard Trade Union Program (Bernard, 1991) for lead officials, evening Certificate courses in the UK and the CLC's five-week residential Labour College of Canada. The Labour College of Canada teaches four courses – labour history, economics, sociology, politics – at a first-year university level in a four-week block. Labour law is now taught as a one-week course in the regions.

Although the Labour College of Canada uses some university educators and takes place in the University of Ottawa, it is a separate entity directly accountable to the CLC. This differs from the Harvard program with its more autonomous structure and from other US college programs and from the adult residential colleges in the UK, such as Ruskin and Northern College. These offer year-long programs and are open to union members. Similar *labour studies* programs can be found in other countries and within some mainstream university offerings (particularly in the US, Australia, New Zealand and

Canada), such as those offered at Athabasca University – although these are open to the general public. In many cases labour studies courses are offered after members have undertaken *tools* and *issues* courses.

Perhaps the most innovative example of a labour studies program offered to union members is the negotiated paid educational leave (PEL) program developed by the Canadian Autoworkers (CAW) and now also offered by the Canadian Union of Postal Workers (CUPW). The core offering is four separate but linked one-week units targeted at all members, not just representatives and activists, and funded by an employer levy negotiated at the bargaining table (the unions retain sole control over content).

The intention of the dedicated *labour studies* courses is to supplement trade union *tools* and *issues* courses with a broader educational program, and in some cases to provide a research basis for union activity. Some universities are linking directly with unions to offer research collaborations (for example, Leeds in the UK) or study and research circles (for example, in Sweden). Although unions are usually represented on the "boards of studies" of the university and college offered *labour studies* programs, they are rarely union controlled in contrast to the union run courses. The variations in the nature, structures and delivery of labour education courses are manifest, and this book provides but a few examples.

One way to think about the differences between these types of courses is to focus on the central purpose and activity of each. *Tools* courses prepare lay representatives, such as shop stewards, for their day-to-day functioning as union representatives. *Issues* courses allow union members, activists and representatives to become more aware of topics such as racism, new management techniques, and particular changes in legislation or union campaigns and then, having considered them, they are likely to develop an action plan to address the issues. Both of these are different from *labour studies* courses that tend to review the contexts within which labour operates, for example the historical, social and political. Labour Studies courses may not result in any immediate impact on day-to-day functioning or on union action plans. The differences between these types of courses are fluid. Some courses will have elements of each type in the one course, for example an introductory course for shop stewards could have a history or political economy component and an issues section. This categorization therefore is suggested to help us understand what is happening in labour education, what unions are offering in core labour education and why. Where unions put their emphasis may vary depending on such factors as the type of union philosophy advocated – business unionism (accommodative/adaptive) versus organizing model (oppositional/militant). The first philosophical approach may result in more emphasis on *tools* and less on *labour studies.*

Curriculum and teaching methods for these core labour education courses have been hotly contested over the years, and have been linked in the assertion that labour education should adopt a "popular education" or "Freirian" approach. In its extreme form, it was argued that courses would have no specific course content, be experientially based and would respond only to the concerns of course participants attending a particular course, and be led by facilitators rather than teachers. All other educational approaches were dismissed as forms of "banking education." While this debate may have been beneficial in reminding labour educators of the importance of democratic participation in the classroom and in the union and the links between the two, it also distracted attention from issues of course content. The need to address some of the key issues facing union members and discuss information that may be outside of their immediate experience needs a planned course content as well as participatory methods. Mike Newman (1993) in the *Third Contract* has discussed the question of what adult educational philosophies and teaching methods are appropriate in different kinds of labour education courses and has shown that a range of different educational approaches can be beneficial.

While methods and curriculum will continue to be an area of debate, Newman's work does illustrate there is no one "correct way" to teach labour education. John McIlroy's chapters in *The Search for Enlightenment* (Simon, 1990) illustrated how some of these concerns can mask a retreat into technical training courses denuded of content and represent a move away from the traditions of workers' education committed to establishing an understanding of political economy among labour activists. It is more common now for unions to offer a range of courses with different foci and to incorporate participatory methods and experiential elements as appropriate: some courses are essentially experiential, others are not. The chapters in this collection illustrate this diversity.

It should also be noted that unions in different countries do run women-only courses and courses targeted at specific groups of members, for example CAW advertises courses for "workers of colour." The intention in these cases is to ensure those attending are not in a minority and any issues that are specific to them are not marginalized.

Other labour education

While *tools, issues* and *labour studies* might describe the majority of labour education, the definitions do not encompass all labour education offerings. Unions are directly involved in a number of membership education programs, some of them with a "basic skills" or vocational purpose. In some cases, union-run literacy and second language courses are tutored by fellow unionists and act as a bridge linking immigrant or illiterate workers to union concerns and publications. Similarly, unions are responsible for a number of worker training programs, which allow the unions to educate workers about union concerns alongside of vocational training. In some countries skilled and professional unions have a long history of union sponsored vocational training and education courses. Unions, including non-craft unions, are becoming much more proactive in responding to company restructuring and deskilling and are arguing for re-skilling, skills recognition and skills profiling, as well as challenging employers to live up to their rhetoric on "pay for knowledge". However, the questions of worker training, worker education or workplace learning (that is training for work) go beyond the scope of this discussion, which is primarily concerned with labour or workers' education – education to support the labour movement not education for work itself. This is a growing area of union educational work and several chapters discuss the increasing union involvement in general membership education and how that fits with core labour education.

In some cases unions have developed a comprehensive and integrated education and training program, such as Britain's UNISON Open College, which includes labour education, basic skills, recognition of prior learning and vocational training opportunities for all union members. In Brazil, *Programa Integrar* offers union sponsored labour education, vocational training and educational opportunities for the unemployed. In other situations unions are engaging in partnered workplace learning programs, partnered with employers or other agencies. Within our review of labour education, a case can be made for including some worker health and safety training in which unions are involved (this should not be confused with union safety representative *tools* training referred to above). These may be joint management courses but they often allow unions to argue for a union view (safe workplace) as opposed to a management view (safe worker) of health and safety. In some cases union-run worker health and safety training has been used as part of union organizing drives.

Nor should we ignore educational provision for full-time officers within our purview of labour education. There has been a growing interest, particularly in Europe, Quebec and Canada generally, in equipping full-time officers (FTOs) with the educational tools needed to conduct union business in a global economy.

Unions have also had some limited involvement in television productions such as "Work Week" or "Working TV" in Canada or the labour education programs broadcast in Britain in the late 1960s and early 1970s. Union representatives participate in television and radio programs in an attempt to present union perspectives, influence public opinion and educate their members. Some unions are actively involved in encouraging schools to broaden their curriculum to include labour issues by providing packages of materials and by training and providing speakers for school visits. Nor should we ignore union sponsored arts and cultural events such as Canada's MayWorks or Manchester, England's labour history museum.

In summary, most core labour education is *tools* training and *issues* courses targeted at union activists, particularly lay representatives (and increasingly union paid staff). In addition, unions and union centrals provide *labour studies* programs, often reserved for those activists who have been through the tools and issues courses, but sometimes targeted at members generally. In some cases public educational institutions or dedicated union training agencies work with unions to provide labour education programs for labour unionists. Unions are also involved in workplace literacy, worker-training programs, and in general education for their members. Unions engage in television broadcasting and arts and cultural events, all of which are targeted at members and do include some elements of labour education. We should remember that most labour learning occurs through workplace union activity itself.

The extent and effectiveness of labour education

It is difficult to present an accurate picture of the extent of labour education in most countries because in many cases there is no consistent statistical data on labour education courses offered and because there is no clear definition of what constitutes labour education. While some labour centrals do collect information on the numbers of courses provided by them or their affiliates, including the number of union members attending, they often do not have the resources to compile statistical reports. There is also no consistency in the reporting of educational provision by affiliates, provincial/regional labour bodies or independent unions. A union at the local or workplace level or a citywide labour council might provide courses or courses may be offered collaboratively with local colleges. They may draw on funds provided locally or nationally. (This question, as it affects Canada, has been explored more fully in Spencer, 1994. For some raw data on Europe see Bridgford & Stirling, 2000.)

There is also the question of what counts as labour education. Does an in-company course offered to union safety committee members, taught by union and management tutors, count as "labour education?" If so, does it still count if supervisors and management committee members are fellow students? Does a two-hour union induction program for new starters count as labour education?

Given these kinds of questions, it is probably of little value to attempt to pin down an accurate statistic of labour education. At best we can "guesstimate" based on the returns to labour centrals, the records of individual unions, and assumptions as to what constitutes "labour education." A list of items to be incorporated within a working definition of core labour education (particularly the *tools, issues* and shorter non-university *labour studies* courses) might include the following:

- Courses lasting at least one half-day (thereby omitting short talks and inductions for new members)
- All weekend, evening and daytime classes
- Courses essentially controlled by the unions and targeted at their members, union representatives and officials
- Courses designed to enhance union effectiveness or develop union consciousness
- All courses for union members except specific "job" (vocational) training (but including courses on negotiating vocational training).

Using this definition and the statistical information available, we can guess that some three percent of union members per year undergo some form of labour education in most Western countries. The participation rate may have been double that two decades earlier, when the economy was more buoyant and release time was more generously legislated (for example in the UK, Australia and New Zealand) or was easier to negotiate (in Canada and the USA). Although unions have been weakened and union density – the percentage of the non-agricultural workforce that is unionized – decreased through the 1990s in most countries (Scandinavia excepted), unions are continuing to give education a high priority. Such a "guesstimate" would, for example, place Canadian and US labour education at a similar percentage level of provision to that in the UK, mainland Europe and Australia (although there is probably less study time per student in Canada, Australia and the US than in the UK). British, Continental European, Australian, Canadian and US levels, however, would be much lower than the level of provision in Scandinavia (approximately 6-10 percent, depending on definitions used), where there are stronger traditions of union and workers' education and different relations between unions and the state than exist in most other Western countries (see Stirling's chapter on European provision).

The extent of labour education varies over time, in some cases just reflecting economic circumstances, in others economic and legal changes. The move to neo-liberal economic policies and globalization of production was accompanied in many countries by attacks on the legal rights to paid educational leave for union representatives (particularly in Europe and Australia/New Zealand where these had been most extensive). These educational rights became increasingly narrowly defined to rights to training for industrial relations purposes; they became more limited in the amount of time allowed, and state funding to support this activity was either cut or abolished altogether (for a review of European experience, see accounts in Bridgford & Stirling, 2000).

How effective is labour education? Since unions invest a lot of time and resources in education, it is clearly important to them. However, other events in a unionist's life, such as a strike or participation in actual negotiations, may provide more important learning opportunities than a union course – no matter how carefully crafted – which may be considered once removed from the actual experience. Nevertheless, unions regard education as underpinning the union effort in the workplace and community. Over the years a number of studies have been conducted in several countries as to the effectiveness of labour education (for sources and data on Canada see Spencer, 1994, Gereluk, 2001, and for the UK see Spencer, 1992). In general studies have found that union members and unions benefit from individuals taking union courses; the courses do help members to become more interested in the union; members are able to make better union decisions as a result of attending union courses; and the courses give members the confidence to take on voluntary positions in the union and to challenge arbitrary management decisions. In addition, union education has been found to bolster members' communal, social and political activity. Labour education does support union activism.

Labour education is essentially education for social purpose. It is not undertaken to earn individualized credit (although credits are now a feature in some countries, students don't enter courses for "credit" but to become better equipped union members) or vocational advantage (again, union courses are now being recognized within some countries vocational qualifications systems, but generally students don't enrol for vocational reasons). Labour education supports union organizational and membership needs. It can also support diversity of opinion within society and social action. For example, even the general educational provision of UNISON has been found to not only benefit the individual members but to feed back into greater activism within the union. Labour education is thus learning for life inside the union and learning for life in general.

REFERENCES

- Bernard, E. (1991). Labour programs: A challenging partnership. *Labour/Le Travail 27*, Spring, 199-207.
- Bridgford, J. & Stirling, J. (Eds.). (2000). *Trade union education in Europe*. Brussels: European Trade Union College.
- Gereluk, W. (2001). *Labour education in Canada today*. Athabasca, AB: Athabasca University.
- Newman, M. (1993). *The third contract: Theory and practice in trade union training*. Sydney: Stewart Victor Publishing.
- Simon, B. (Ed.). (1990). *The search for enlightenment: The working class and adult education in the twentieth century*. London: Lawrence and Wishart.
- Spencer, B. (1994). Educating union Canada. *Canadian Journal for the Study of Adult Education. 8*(2) 45-64. (Revised version in Poonwassie, D. & A. (Eds.). (2001). *Fundamentals of adult education*. Toronto: Thompson Educational Publishing, pp.214-231.)
- Spencer, B. (1992). Labour education in the UK and Canada: What do workers do and what should they be offered on union courses? *Canadian and International Education 20*(2), 55-68.

UNIT I
PERSPECTIVES ON PROVISION

John Stirling opens this section with a review of the state of labour education in 15 European Economic Area countries. He locates the developments in labour education within the historic political changes experienced by European unions and concludes by summarizing union education responses to the new Europe. He argues that labour education in Europe is rebounding from two decades of decline but questions what has been lost in the process.

Linda Cooper provides a detailed insider account of the establishment and progress of South Africa's Development Institute for the Training, Support and Education of Labour (Ditsela). This chapter is a valuable insight into the challenges facing union learning when unions move from a position of revolutionary opposition to fulfilling a new role as bargaining agents within a liberal democracy. She questions what role union education can play in aiding the least organized and most exploited workers.

Tom Nesbit reviews the educational provision for full-time officers (FTOs) in the UK, USA and Canada within the context of overall labour education policy and the changing nature of work. Tom notes that most FTOs come from within the union membership, and he discusses the limited educational provision available to FTOs. His chapter provides a powerful rationale for a greater emphasis on education for labour's professionals, particularly in their roles as "administrators" and "analysts."

Rita Kwok Hoi Yee explains the different influences on the concept "workers' rights" as it is understood in China. She considers that the social cohesion evident in both Confucian and Marxist writings ill prepares workers for the challenges involved in a move towards a liberal market economy. She concludes by asserting the relevance of experientially based education methods for Chinese workers.

2

Trade Union Education in Europe: Emerging from the Gloom

JOHN STIRLING

The focus of this chapter is on the countries of the European Economic Area, which effectively excludes the former Soviet bloc nations with their inevitably different approaches to trade unionism and trade union education. Even within this restricted geographical framework there are strong differences between countries in Southern Europe that have emerged from dictatorships to rebuild their trade union movements and those in the Nordic countries characterized by long periods of stable social democratic government and high levels of trade union membership. Nevertheless, the data from the 15 national reports, which provide the empirical basis for this analysis, suggests that there are common themes deriving from common problems.

In what follows I will briefly review the context in which post-war trade union education for union representatives developed in Europe and indicate the importance of adult education traditions, especially in northern Europe, and the relationship between politics and pragmatism in the content and delivery of education. The next section will contextualize current developments by reviewing patterns of post-war changes in trade unions and their relationship to education programs. The third section will analyse current trends in Europe through an examination of the key issues of pedagogy and content. From this discussion it will be clear that trade union education in Europe has suffered from two decades of hostile attacks and increasing pressures for change. It is now emerging from this gloom with greater self-reliance and professionalism, but might this be at the cost at the deep-rooted values of solidarity and collectivism?

Building the foundations

The development of education programs for trade unionists can only be understood in the context of the development of trade unions themselves and the debates that surrounded them. Furthermore, education as a distinct activity is influenced by national traditions and debates relating to appropriate educational strategies and pedagogies. Inevitably, both these areas are characterized by different political approaches and these have inevitably coloured the different approaches to trade union education across Europe.

In the Nordic countries and the UK, relatively early historical settlements were made by the unions with national labour and social democratic parties. These have remained relatively stable although there are inevitably exceptions such as the split in the social democratic party in Finland in the 1950s and 1960s that led to parallel political divisions in the trade union movement. Similar "settlements" occurred in Belgium and the Netherlands but these were politically more complex given the importance of cultural, linguistic and religious differences. The significance of this for the education of trade unionists was the relative lack of schism between trade unions wishing to transmit particular ideologies to their membership. This is not to argue that trade union education programs were devoid of political content or that there were not alternatives to the dominance of social democracy. Rather it is to contrast these developments to those elsewhere in Europe where ideological divisions shaped education provision. In this context, the method of delivery of education programs also becomes a critical issue.

A defining feature of trade union education in the Nordic countries has been its relationship to adult education more generally and to the use of adult education programs as a characteristic feature of the national democratic process. The implication of this is that trade union education is "owned" and shaped by the participants and that learning strategies are necessarily participative and student-centred. However, while this "ownership" might be clearly expressed in the classroom via study circles where participants can dictate the flow of learning, the trade union confederations also developed clear programs. The dominance of single trade union centres and the developing institutional links with folk high schools and Workers' Educational Associations encouraged this development of stable, structured programs of education. In essence, the "method" was part of the "message" in its encouragement of democratic participation and collective learning.

In the countries of Europe where the relationship between dominant trade union central confederations and single social democratic parties was not so clearly established, trade union education necessarily developed different traditions (Bridgford & Stirling, 1988). Communist, socialist and Catholic linked confederations were recruiting members not simply in relation to skill or industry but also in the context of political affiliations. In this respect, education programs needed to reinforce the identity of particular confederations as against others and to transmit an ideology to leading cadres. This was reinforced by often-unstable political climates that descended into civil war and dictatorship in some countries. Furthermore, adult education traditions were not firmly entrenched nor had they created institutional structures in the way they had in the Nordic countries. This led to traditions of centralized delivery of education programs with little, if any, State support and with a strong focus on content rather than method. Questions of content also dominated debate in other European countries where political conflicts were less prevalent and where workplace trade unionism was a central focus. In such circumstances, the clash between capital and labour is transmuted from class struggle in the political arena to delivering more prosaic outcomes for members. This provides the context to a debate typified by that in the UK between the provision of practical skills or "competencies" and encouraging the development of a more general political awareness (McIlroy, 1999).

The issues of content and method are, clearly, defining features of trade union education programs and there are marked contrasts in developments across Europe. However, general statements will necessarily neglect particular national circumstances and it is equally the case that all trade union movements were faced with similar challenges in relation to the delivery of education programs. In this respect it is only possible to identify dominant features and trends in a comparative study. The next section deals with key issues in post-war development.

Periods of change

The development of trade union education is inextricably linked to more general changes in trade union activity, which are in turn related to developments in national industrial relations frameworks. In the broadest sense the post-war era can be periodized into the years from 1945 until the mid-1970s; from then until the mid 1980s and from then until the turn of the century. We are again challenged with exceptions but some general trends approximating to these periods can be identified.

The immediate post-war period is characterized by a period of economic restructuring and changes in the labour markets that were characterized by significant expansions in public sector and white-collar employment. Trade union response to these changes eventually led to the consolidation and expansion of membership. Industrial relations frameworks were also being re-established or built anew and of critical significance was the establishment of "dual systems" of industrial relations in countries such as France, Belgium, Germany and the Netherlands where works councils were given representational functions at the workplace. This had an important impact on trade union education, as legal rights to time off work for training became focused on works councillors rather than trade unions, and curriculum content became focused on the role of the works councillor. Similar strategies developed elsewhere and, as McIlroy comments in relation to the UK, "trade union education was now explicitly and forcefully redefined as training shop stewards in workplace industrial relations" (1999, p. 49). In the Nordic countries, trade unions generally maintained their traditions of strong, independent representation at the workplace and a broader approach to education remained entrenched.

These developments reached their highpoint in the second period, mid 1970s to mid 1980s, when a resurgence of trade union militancy and the response of social democratic governments led to the establishment of legal frameworks for trade union and works council education. Thus, for much of the next decade there was legislation on trade union rights across Europe that included new rights or improved arrangements for time off work for training and new sources of funding. For example, new legislation or collective agreements in relation to works councillor training were introduced in Austria (1974), Belgium (1985), France (1982 and 1985), Germany (1972), and the Netherlands (1971 and 1979). Rights in relation to trade union training were introduced, for example, in Denmark (1973), Sweden (1974) and the UK (1976).

Visser argues that "the 1980s stand out as a unique period of union decline in post-war Europe" (1994, p. 82). Although the pattern of decline was uneven and the Nordic countries were still able to stave off the worst effects, this inevitably had its effect on the institutional arrangements supporting trade union education. In this respect the most dramatic action was the withdrawal of funding by the Swedish government in 1991 leading to a decline in average annual numbers attending basic LO trade union education programs from around 20-30,000 to 4-5,000 by the end of the 1990s (Unden, 2000). There were also continuous reductions in grants and support in both Norway and Finland throughout the 1990s. In Germany and the UK there were also attempts to restrict trade union education either through legal attacks by the employers or through hostile governments withdrawing support.

Elsewhere in Europe, changes in bargaining arrangements or reform of union organization were having more positive results for trade union education but in national situations where provision was often already weak. In Greece, for example, the 1990s saw strong attempts to reform trade union structure and increase effectiveness, and in 1990 the national confederation established an Institute of Labour (INE) to support the development of trade union education although with little legal support or funding it remains fragmented (Kouzis, 2000). Italy saw a number of attempts by the different central confederations to work together and respond to changes in bargaining arrangements. In particular, the growth of workplace representatives (Rappresentanze Sindacali Unitarie) necessitated new training arrangements and these were supported by national collective agreements in 1993 and 1998 which allowed time off work for union activity generally but could also be utilised to support training. In Ireland, the voluntarist nature of industrial relations which had supported the expansion of trade union education from the 1970s found expression in a Code of Practice in 1990 which established rights to time off work, although they often remain difficult to implement (O'Brien, 2000).

By the end of the 1990s trade union education across Europe faced a number of challenges. Declining membership, reduced subscription income and forced cuts in training budgets. These funding problems were reinforced in a number of countries, particularly in Northern Europe, where previously sympathetic State funding regimes and national legislation had been challenged, narrowed in focus or withdrawn. This was reinforced by employer hostility to supporting trade union education and, in particular, by a growing resistance to paid time off work. Changes in industrial relations frameworks and generalized shifts from centralized to decentralized collective bargaining arrangements also posed new training challenges as workplace representatives required new skills. Equally, shifts in labour markets and the reorganization of work demanded new responses. These challenges are inevitably also opportunities and reviews of education provision were widespread across Europe by the turn of the century.

There's a new world somewhere

The restructuring of trade union education in Europe from its highpoint in the 1970s has focused on the key areas of program content and mode of delivery. This in a context where trade unions have sought to "professionalize" their provision in response to restricted funding and changing demands from union representatives. This has led to conflicting pressures for education to be "demand-led" to ensure financial viability as well as responsiveness to rapid changes and a need for strategic planning to ensure that education is part of a co-ordinated program of development. One clear example might be to contrast training in organizing and recruitment to meet organizational needs for membership growth with membership demands for training in new management strategies. The obvious response is to do both but unions are faced with making real decisions about priorities in relation to their resources.

It is in program content that new areas of development are clearly apparent and four have emerged of particular significance: workplace organizing, personal skills development, the changing nature of work and the European Union. Before looking at these in detail it is important to make a more general point. The shift in trade union education towards skills-based competencies and away from a broader, political, education is now well established. The key reasons for this are the decline in ideological differences between national trade union confederations, the strictures of laws (or collective agreements) that focus on "relevant" training or limit provision to the narrow remit of works councils and, finally, the strategic priorities of the trade unions themselves. This is not to suggest that broader issues have disappeared completely and they remain where countries have structured programs that provide training over time and where representatives are expected to develop their knowledge in stages. They are also at least implicit in new programs that confront questions of globalization and the changing nature of work.

In relation to the four issues identified above it is self-evident that organizing and recruitment is not a new issue for trade union education. However, consistent growth in the post-war period saw trade unions in much of Europe as almost passive recipients of new members. The reversal was initially matched by an equally passive response but this has shifted as trade unions have developed strategies to develop themselves as active agents in their own recruitment, particularly in new areas of the labour market. This activity has necessarily been supported by education programs that focus on organizing potential new members. In the UK, where membership decline was dramatic, organizing models from the USA and Australia have been influential in developing new approaches (see chapter by Widenor and Feekin). This has led to the establishment of an Organizing Academy and also the extension of training to representatives in a program known as "winning the organized workplace." These strategies inevitably place increased demands on training to support representatives who will be required to develop new skills in communication and campaigning. Whilst the British TUC has been prominent in developing this side of its education program other trade union centres in Europe have been doing the same.

The changing nature of work has preoccupied trade unions as they seek to develop appropriate responses and incorporate them into education programs. Two aspects of this have emerged as particularly significant in education programs. First, there is basic knowledge provision designed to help representatives understand the changes occurring in global capitalism and its consequences for local labour markets and the organization of work. This educational development is consistent across the European trade unions with program developments in, for example, Italy, Austria and Norway. In Austria the central confederation (OGB) focuses on providing "information and explanations" but also building practical projects to reinforce basic ideas of solidarity but at a global as well as local and national level (Lackinger, 2000). The "Channel 99" program in Norway focused on the relationship between changes at work and their effect on society more generally (Birkeland, 2000). In Sweden, the confederation covering professional and white-collar workers (TCO) has launched a general educational campaign on changes in working life and how they affect the individual. They are particularly concerned to analyze flexible working patterns and develop appropriate trade union responses (Danvind & Mortvik, 1996). Secondly, trade unions are increasingly drawn into "partnerships" or "social dialogue" with employers in response to these changes. Thus, partnership has become a feature of education programs in the UK and Ireland and new training courses in countries such as Italy and Portugal also emphasize the centrality of participation and the importance of developing a social dialogue with employers.

The third area of content development relates to personal skills. In a sense, these have always been a part of trade union education programs given that, for example, communicating effectively is an essential part of negotiating. However, what is new is the stress on the individual and their own development and the importance of such skills for the management of the trade union as an organization. Although some of the focus of these education programs has been on full time officials of trade unions they are also available to workplace representatives. One major area of growth has inevitably been in the use of computer skills with training available in most countries. In Germany, for example, computer skills training now comprises the second largest part of the national confederation's (DGB) training provision. In addition a multimedia centre has been established which offers basic skills training and then provides for the development of an electronic curriculum and skills in using the Internet for research and communication (Romer-Karrasch et. al. 2000). Alongside skills in the use of new technologies there is a strong emphasis on the professional management of trade unions. This is enhanced through personal development in areas such as communications, team building, leadership and interpersonal skills. In the Netherlands, the unions have been concerned to put together education packages that serve activists personal interests in basic areas such as oral and written communication and also enhance employability (Slomp, 2000). There has also been a concern to develop vocational training for representatives and members in areas that were previously left to the public education system or employers. In Finland (Tuomisto, 2000) and the UK the respective unions representing low paid public sector employees have both developed vocational training to enhance the personal skills of members and enable them to participate in an education system that has often excluded them – particularly where they have been female, atypical workers.

The final area of development in terms of content is in relation to the European Union. To a large degree this is an inevitable development as countries join the European Union and trade union movements need to respond to the general economic and political changes as well as to the specific details of new labour legislation that now derives from the Commission in areas such as equal opportunities, health and safety and working time. There is also important institutional and financial support for the development of trade union education programs from the European Union. The European Trade Union College was established a decade ago to provide training for trade union tutors in European issues, produce training materials and provide support for cross Europe training projects (Bridgford, 1996). Financial support from the European Union has been utilised by national trade union movements in a number of ways and it has proved particularly important for unions in southern Europe with less developed training programs. Funding can be utilised to fund gaps in provision in relation to specific areas such as the education of women or young people or in particular geographical areas. Cross-Europe partnerships can also find funding for the development of particular training projects that allows for joint seminars or the publication of materials. Finally, the European Union has been an important source of funding for the development of European Works Council training (see the chapter by Miller).

In terms of national training programs, provision has been particularly intense in periods up to and immediately following applications for European Union membership in countries such as Sweden, Spain, Portugal and Finland. Once countries have become established members of the European Union, education tends to shift its focus to European Institutions and European Union policies. In Italy, for example, the confederations provide courses on European monetary union, European social policy, women in Europe, the expansion of the European Union and also cover developments in particular economic sectors. In Greece, the European Union has provided a very significant base for the development of trade union education in three ways. Firstly, the inclusion of a European dimension on core course programs; secondly, the development of joint programs in Greece with other European organizations and thirdly through the participation of Greek trade unionists on international programs. Whilst the figure is likely to be exceptional and related to the low level of other funding Kouzis (2000) estimates that 25 percent of expenditure on trade union training in Greece is now financed from the European Union.

Strategies for delivering education

Issues of pedagogy are moving from longstanding developments in classroom learning strategies that have now become universal. The shift to active, participant-based learning strategies using a variety of methods has occurred across Europe and has been accepted in those countries where more traditional, expert-led, practices had predominated. Key issues now relate to the structure of course programs, distance and electronic delivery and accreditation.

In terms of program structure, this is partly dependent on the relationships between national union centres, individual unions and other providing bodies. There is a general tendency for decentralization in provision so that individual unions commonly provide basic programs and confederations or public education institutions provide more specialized courses. This is not always the case, particularly where unions are small and under resourced or there is a tradition of centralized provision. This decentralization is a challenge to longstanding structured programs and is a response to delivering demand-led shorter course programs. In Denmark, for example, whilst a clear program remains in place there is a move away from a systematic "building-block" approach towards shorter course modules from which students make their own choices (Hansen and Sommer, 2000). This leads to the second point in relation to accreditation of programs and links with academic institutions. This is not the place to review the debate but it should be noted that the question of accreditation is not uncontroversial given that it raises questions about co-operative and collective learning and notions of "pass and fail." It might also be challenged where accreditation is a necessary corollary of funding. On the other hand there are arguments that accreditation can accommodate collective learning and values, that it recognizes achievement, provides a benchmark for establishing quality standards and coincides with notions of personal development.

In some countries, such as France, there are longstanding relationships with academic institutions. The French trade unions have a long association with labour institutes in universities which were established in Strasbourg in 1955 and in Sceaux in 1959 and which provide courses nationally and with eight other institutes which operate at a regional level (Geoffroy, 2000). In a number of other countries there are equally longstanding arrangements although they are generally less systematic and institutionalized than the French. In Ireland there is a systematic, staged program of development involving academic institutions in accreditation. Trade union representatives will complete introductory courses proved and certificated by their own union or the Irish national confederation, progress to a Certificate in Trade Union Studies accredited by the Irish National Council for Educational Awards and move on to complete a diploma and finally a degree accredited by University College Dublin (O'Brien, 2000). Another approach has been adopted by the DGB confederation in Germany where its independent Education Institute has gained a quality standard through certification under the international ISO 9000.

Finally, in terms of program delivery, there is a considerable amount of development across Europe in the use of electronic media to support distance-learning programs. In Norway, for example, which has a tradition of distance learning (the Peoples' Correspondence School was established in 1947), programs are being adapted to be used through information technology whilst also seeking to maintain combinations of group working, projects, study circles and opportunities for debate (Birkeland, 2000). In Italy, CISL has developed a strong telematic network. A "First Class" program manages discussion forums, information exchange and on-line tutoring whilst interactive programs have been developed through the "Mercurio" project. These electronic communication methods have also provided for links between trainers and allowed task groups to develop new teaching materials on-line. In effect, all of the European countries are exploring electronic communications as a way of delivering material that is cost effective, flexible for the students and innovative (see Taylor's chapter for a broader discussion on on-line learning).

Conclusion

The suggestion in the title to this chapter is that trade union education in Europe is "emerging from the gloom." There can be little doubt that the well-documented retreat of trade unionism in general has had a substantial impact on education provision. When budgets are cut, training is one of the first things to go. Challenging time off work provisions and reducing resources are both easy targets for employers and hostile governments. This is not to discount the resilience of trade unions in delivering programs, particularly where they have been deeply embedded in national culture and practice. However, it has been hard for newly emerging democracies in parts of Southern Europe to establish programs or for them to be sustained where confederations and trade unions have been divided. The question is, are there enough bright lights to dissipate the gloom?

Many European trade union centres have taken the opportunity to review their programs both as a response to a declining resource and as a valued asset central to a strategic response to rapid changes at work. Reviews of education programs were common across Europe from the early 1990s onwards resulting in, for example, new systems being established in Denmark in 1999, a new program of education development by SAK in Finland in 1998, Institutes responsible for Labour Education being established by CGIL in Italy in 1995 and in Greece in 1990 and a review in Ireland resulting in the publication of *Learning for a Changing World* in 1995. Perhaps the archetypal development might be the establishment of FNV Formaat in the Netherlands in 1998 (Slomp, 2000). This is an independent institute responsible for its own funding which is gradually taking over training provision from the private sector unions in the FNV (the largest Dutch confederation) and is involved in running training programs for union officers, works councillors, health and safety representatives and European Works Councillors. In effect, the outcome of retrenchment has been the "professionalization" of trade union education. This is also reflected in the content focus on business education, works council training, partnerships with employers and personal development.

For some, these conclusions might deepen the gloom as they seek indications of the radical, collective strengths of trade union education that had a broadly defined political dimension as well as the focus on skills development. There are two responses to this. Firstly, that learning strategies based on co-operation and participation that empowers participants are now entrenched as "the" trade union education method. The ubiquity of such approaches conceals their importance and the resistance to change that had to be overcome. Secondly, the challenges posed by changes in capital inevitably draw a political response from labour that is becoming embedded in education programs. New programs emphasize an active agenda for trade unionists in response to changes at work. New approaches to organizing have the effect of raising precisely the questions of the 1960s and 1970s about workers controlling their unions through their strength at the workplace. Globalization raises questions of labour internationalism that had been lost to the rhetoric of the conference hall and electronic communications provide one means of developing cross-national solidarity. Two decades ago little trade union education would look beyond national boundaries; in Europe today there is little alternative but to do so. Neither, finally, is there any reason why the radical should not be delivered professionally.

Acknowledgements: In addition to those reports cited directly in the references this chapter has relied heavily on the 15 national research studies that were produced as part of the survey of trade union education in Europe undertaken by the European Trade Union College. The author would like to thank Jeff Bridgford, Director of the College, and the authors of these reports.

Editors note: An abbreviated version of all the "country" reports listed in these references can be found in Bridgford, J. & Stirling, J. (2000) *Trade union education in Europe.* Brussels: European Trade Union College.

REFERENCES

- Birkeland, E. S. (2000). *Norway,* Unpublished. Brussels: European Trade Union College.
- Bridgford, J. (1996). *Trade union education in Europe: The role of the European trade union college.* In E. Gabaglio & R. Hoffmann (Eds.), *European Trade Union Yearbook 1995,* Brussels: European Trade Union Institute.
- Bridgford, J. & Stirling, J. (1988). *Ideology or pragmatism? Trade union education in France and Britain, Industrial Relations Journal, 19*(3), 234-43.
- Danvind, E-M. & Mortvik, R. (1996). *Learn for your life.* Stockholm, TCO.
- Geoffroy, M. (2000). *France.* Unpublished report. Brussels: European Trade Union College.
- Hansen, L. & Sommer, F. M. (2000). *Denmark.* Unpublished report. Brussels: European Trade Union College.
- Kouzis, Y. (2000). *Greece.* Unpublished report. Brussels: European Trade Union College.
- Lackinger. F-J. (2000). *Austria.* Unpublished report. Brussels: European Trade Union College.
- McIlroy, J. (1999). Making trade unionists: The politics of pedagogy, 1945-79. In A. Cambpell, N. Fishman, & J. McIlroy (Eds.), *British trade unions and industrial politics (Vol. 1).* Ashgate: Aldershot.
- O'Brien, G. (2000). *Ireland.* Unpublished report. Brussels: European Trade Union College.
- Romer-Karrasch, M., Gehrmann, A. & Hanns, W. (2000). *Germany* Unpublished report. Brussels: European Trade Union College.
- Slomp, H. (2000). *The Netherlands.* Unpublished report. Brussels: European Trade Union College.
- Tuomisto, J. (2000). *Finland.* Unpublished report. Brussels: European Trade Union College.
- Unden, T. (2000). *Sweden.* Unpublished report. Brussels: European Trade Union College.
- Visser, J. (1994). European trade unions: The transition years. In R. Hyman, & A. Ferner (Eds.), *New frontiers in European industrial relations.* Oxford: Blackwell.

3

Union Education in the New South African Democracy

LINDA COOPER

Ditsela, oh! Ditsela
Remember the workers all the time.
Ditsela, oh! Ditsela
Yours name brings hope to workers
Pathway for the workers' development, Pathways for the workers upliftment
Workers have waited so long for this road
They have died while paving this way.
Ditsela, oh! Ditsela
The one who holds the light, The one who's going to plant the knowledge
Remember that you are doing it for workers
Universities are built for academics
Remember – you're the light and wisdom
For the workers.
Extract from: *Ditsela! Ditsela* – A praise poem presented by worker poet, Nise
Malange to the launch of Ditsela, November 1996

As excitement mounted with the approach of the first, non-racial democratic elections in South Africa's history, the largest of the trade union federations – COSATU (Congress of South African Trade Unions) – was engaged in intense discussions around the establishment of a new, national body to support and develop trade union education. Cosatu anticipated that for the first time, trade unions would be able to make a claim on public funding for their education work, but such support would be conditional on the major federations co-operating in one, joint project. The Congress therefore entered discussions with the more Black Consciousness aligned NACTU (National Council of Trade Unions) and the historically "white" and conservative Fedsal (now Fedusa – Federation of Unions of South Africa). After two years, the Development Institute for Training, Support and Education for Labour – Ditsela – was launched on November 29, 1996.

Ditsela's establishment was supported by the Cosatu and Fedusa, but ultimately not by Nactu[2]. Cosatu was interested in rebuilding the labour movement's capacity to respond to the major changes underway in the country. From the early 1990s, and particularly after the first democratic elections in 1994, there had been a steady flow of Cosatu leadership out of the unions and into political office. This and other factors left its affiliates struggling to deal with a range of new and complex issues that began to emerge through engagement in tripartite negotiations and in high-level policy debates. There was a strong belief that a major education initiative was required to build the Cosatu's capacity to play a proactive role in the new, democratic South Africa.

For Fedusa, on the other hand – a relatively new federation emerging from a history of conservative, white trade unionism where little if any trade union education took place – Ditsela offered the possibility of building education capacity for the first time, which could support new organizational strategies to broaden its membership.

This chapter will review the work of Ditsela over the first four years of its existence and will analyze its achievements and problems, and the challenges it faces as a major actor in the field of South African labour education at the beginning of the twenty-first century. It will argue that in many ways, Ditsela both reflects, and seeks to address, the major fault-lines running through trade union education within the context of a labour movement undergoing a significant transition in its identity and politics.

Ditsela: pathways to a strong labour movement[3]

At its first Educators Conference held six months after its establishment, Ditsela formally adopted its Vision and Principles for trade union education. In important ways, these echoed the values of earlier, radical education traditions within South Africa's labour movement, with their strong emphasis on worker control and the independence of trade union education. But they also reflected the political and identity shifts taking place within the labour movement in post-apartheid South Africa. As the largest of the federations, Cosatu, assumed the role of ally of the new, democratic government and that of a major player in economic and social policy formulation (Cooper, 1998a).

Ditsela's vision was to play a "dynamic part in the building and maintenance of a strong, independent labour movement" and "make a critical contribution to the development of membership, representatives, leadership and trade union staff into creative, critical and effective trade unionists and citizens who transform society with other organs of civil society." (Ditsela, 1997b, p.8) It would operate according to the following principles:

NACTU's refusal to become involved in Ditsela is related its unhappiness over the formula for trade union representation on the Board of Ditsela, as well as concerns over who would control the content and politics of trade union education. The attempt to draw in Nactu is ongoing.

[3] The "motto" of Ditsela. Ditsela means "pathways" in Sotho, a South African language.

- The aims and programs of trade union education are based on the aims, objectives, needs, principles, policies and values of the trade unions;
- Overall responsibility for and control of trade union education rests with the trade union movement;
- The main purpose of trade union education is to build and strengthen trade unions as collective organizations, serving the interests of workers at all levels;
- Trade union education is not neutral, but supports the change and development of society in the interests of working class people;
- Trade union education, whilst contributing to the development of individuals, primarily focuses on the collective needs of workers and the organization;
- There should be a gender balance in all trade union activities;
- The methods used in trade union are participative, democratic and collective;
- Trade union education is independent from employers, government and donors;
- Equal access to trade union education should be provided, including to disadvantaged sectors. (Ditsela, 1997b, p.7)

Ditsela aimed to help develop a systematic framework for trade union education that would bring together the efforts of all groups providing labour education, including federations and their affiliates as well as labour service organizations (LSOs)[4]. It aimed to become the leading centre for the design and delivery of trade union education programs and an innovator in the areas of trade union education policy, approaches and methods.

During the first few months of Ditsela's existence, it was thrust into an energetic campaign of workshops around the country to educate workers and union members on the provisions of the new Labour Relations Amendment Act, which for the first time formally secured the right of all workers to form trade unions, negotiate, and strike, and which established a labour relations framework as progressive – if not more so – than any in the industrialized world. But soon Ditsela began the slow and painstaking task of building a more sustainable program of education work, and a year later, four key areas of work had emerged: education programs, networking, support for trade union education, and resources and information.[5]

---

[4] Many LSOs were established during the 1980s and played a key education role in trade union capacity-building. In recent years however, many have been weakened or forced to close due to loss of funding or experienced staff.

[5] Ditsela works with a relatively small complement of its own staff and uses contract educators, researchers and consultants.

Education programs

Ditsela has sought to strike a balance between, first, delivering its own education programs and developing capacity of unions to offer their own education; and second, between courses that focus on skills development and those that develop broader theoretical and social understanding. It has developed a model which includes five year-long, Advanced courses in Labour Law, Organization Development (OD) and Management of Trade Unions, Trade Union Education, Trade Unions Studies (focusing on developing a broad understanding of political economy), and Trade Union Studies for Women (similar content but with a strong gender perspective). The model also includes many shorter courses – often delivered regionally – and some of which are intended to lay a basis for progression to advanced courses.

Networking

Ditsela's Educator Conferences[6] – which draw together worker educators, trade union educators, labour service organizations and university-based labour educators – aim to play an important role in providing a space for reflection on trade union education; building a coherent and united approach and common direction; and energizing and celebrating trade union education. (Ditsela, 1999, p.24).

The first Ditsela Educators' Conference was held in 1997, with the theme Building a Workers' Education Movement; it focused on building unity of purpose and structures of co-operation and networking. The 1998 Conference, New Ways of Seeing, New Ways of Doing, focused not only on the task of rebuilding union education, but also on transforming it by bringing in new ideas and methods. The theme of the 1999 Conference was Reflect, Refocus, Regenerate and represented an attempt to reclaim the history and identity of trade union education.

Ditsela has been involved in establishing a network of trade union educators and LSOs in order to improve collaboration and, in particular, to help LSOs tackle the loss of funding which has severely affected their work since 1994. The first Ditsela conference also identified the need to deepen ties with unions in "the South" – Latin America, Asia and elsewhere in Africa – and over the past three years, Ditsela has taken this seriously.[7]

Support

Ditsela has been conscious of the danger of "substituting" itself for trade unions' own education, and it has put in the foreground building the capacity of unions to deliver their own education. Their efforts have taken the form of

---

[6]   Annual 1997 to 1999, now bi-annual.

[7]   Ditsela has affiliated to the International Federation of Workers' Education Associations; it has begun to collaborate with other African trade union bodies; and staff have been on exchange visits to North and South America.

facilitator development; training and support of educator staff; internships; materials development; and assisting trade unions with designing education programs and building organizational structures.

Resources and Information

The Ditsela Resource Centre collects materials nationally and internationally, and responds to information requests from trade unions and other organizations. Ditsela also publishes an education newsletter, Pathways, to act as a forum for news and debate on worker education.

Ditsela has placed strong emphasis on research to assist itself, and labour education more generally, to plan ahead more systematically and coherently. Research projects under its auspices have included:

- An international, comparative analysis of trade union systems and forms of accreditation;

- "Mapping" the strengths and weaknesses of trade union education in South Africa;

- Research into the shifting nature of trade union work and roles

- Developing a directory of Labour Service Organizations.

Achievements and critical challenges facing Ditsela

Ditsela's work has begun to bear fruit in the form of systematic education research and planning, the delivery of ongoing and sustainable education programs, attempts to build co-ordination between different levels of providers, and some proactive, innovative and creative education projects. Ditsela has also begun to give labour education a national profile and a firmer sense of identity.

However, its ongoing reports note several key problems and challenges. Participation from women trade unionists continues to be low[8]. Participants attending courses are often not those who have been targeted; there is a problem of dropouts from courses; and provision continues to be concentrated in metropolitan areas rather than in smaller towns and rural areas where the need is always greater.[9] There is a tendency for unions to expect Ditsela to meet all their education needs; a 1998 research report found that:

---

[8] Between 1996 and 1998, the proportion of women trade unionists on Ditsela courses ranged between 15.5% and 27% (Ditsela 1998a & 1998e). In 1998 Ditsela adopted a gender policy requiring 25% of places to be reserved for women participants, and gender issues to be integrated into all courses.

[9] As early as 1997 Ditsela attempted to widen delivery to smaller centres but experienced difficulties, mainly a lack of resources. It hopes that the integration process currently underway between Ditsela and three Workers Colleges (based in Cape Town, Port Elizabeth and Durban) will help to strengthen local/regional delivery.

In the eyes of the interviewees Ditsela would solve all of their education problems. When they were asked what they would like Ditsela to do, most of them said that it should meet all the needs that they had identified for the union... (Ditsela, 1998d, p.19)

At the 1998 Educator Conference the question was raised: "Is Ditsela now a substitute for federation education at national and regional levels?" (Ditsela, 1998e, p.7). From time to time, LSOs have complained that they are not drawn on enough by Ditsela, and that Ditsela is taking over their traditional areas of work.

It is, however, important to view these issues against the broader backdrop of organizational weaknesses within the trade union movement generally, and lack of education capacity in particular. A 1997 Ditsela-commissioned survey of trade union education needs and capacities reported that union education is very weak generally, particularly in regions where it is needed most; union education often reaches only very small numbers, with little attention being paid to membership education; most education officials are new – less than two years in their posts – and they feel that their educator roles are poorly defined and that there is a lack of support from top leadership for labour education; finally, there is huge variation in capacity – between federations, and within federations – making it very difficult for an institution such as Ditsela to identify common needs (Ditsela, 1997a).[10]

A 1998 regional survey of trade union education (Ditsela, 1998b) confirmed this picture. It found that in the regions, there was very little substantial education delivery; that there was a lack of education structures, policies and resources; an almost universal lack of capacity to plan, monitor and evaluate education programs; a lack of capacity in methodological, facilitation and materials development skills; a worrying increase in the amount of shop-steward training being carried out by management and private consultants; and a sidelining of gender issues. The 1998 Educators Conference also heard that LSOs were facing a serious funding crisis, that unions are reliant on external funding, and often they have no dedicated amount for education in their budgets.

A 1998 Conference document identified several key issues facing Ditsela. Two of these will be focused on to illustrate how the difficulties and challenges of Ditsela reflect broader themes and dilemmas facing South African labour education currently. The first issue was referred to in a conference resolution as the need to "deepen commitment to common principles and vision based on working class politics, whilst being flexible enough to accommodate differences within the constituency." The second issue was referred to as the challenge of maintaining a collective approach "in the face of trends towards individualism and encroachment by 'non worker friendly' agencies into the field of union education." (Ditsela 1998f, p.13)

---

[10] When this report was tabled at Conference, delegates said "the situation is actually worse than the presentation indicated" (Ditsela, 1997b, p.6).

Common principles whilst accommodating differences

A 2000 Ditsela pamphlet, dedicated to "Challenging our prejudice and abuse," declares:

> We are black; We are white; We are amaZulu; We are baSotho; We are dancers; We are gay; We are straight; We are ZCC; We are Muslim; We are HIV+; We are raped; We are loved; We are banktellers; We are farmworkers; We are all workers.......

It asks: "How can we celebrate our differences and use them to build a strong, healthy movement and society? To address these, Ditsela has adopted four critical themes that weave through all our work: gender equality, unity and diversity, HIV/AIDS, rape." Ditsela's 1999 conference also emphasized that its history is not monolithic: "We are also interested in different histories and cultures of the labour movement" (Ditsela, 1999, p.2).

The issue of diversity – political, ideological, and cultural – is an issue labour movements elsewhere in the world have grappled with extensively. In South Africa, however, much effort has been spent in overcoming apart-heid-imposed divisions and building unity and non-racialism in the struggle against apartheid. Today, democratic organizations are grappling almost for the first time with how to openly confront and work with difference, whilst at the same time maintain solidarity.

The two federations whose representatives sit on the governing board of Ditsela,[11] and whose members comprise the overwhelming majority of the participants on its programs, have deeply differing histories and traditions. Costasu, the largest of the trade union federations in South Africa, historically played the leading role in the radical movement of internal opposition to the apartheid regime; in the post-apartheid period, it has remained explicitly com-mitted to socialism and condemns the increasing shift of the African National Congress (ANC) government towards neo-liberal economic policies – while continuing to re-affirm its support as an "alliance partner" of government. Fedusa on the other hand emerged historically from a conservative tradition of trade unionists who, under apartheid, worked (willingly or unwillingly) within a bureaucratic and racist "industrial conciliation system," who were committed to opposing communism and supporting free enterprise, and are still strongly committed to non-political trade unionism (Davies, O'Meara & Dlamini, 1984, 250-55).

Political differences between representatives of these two federations have caused ongoing tension within the Ditsela Board. Fedusa has complained that Ditsela facilitators are politically biased towards Cosatu, and has accused Ditsela of being "the training arm of Cosatu" (Ditsela, 1998c; 2000a); it has asked Ditsela to support efforts to build Fedusa's own programs, rather than

---

[11] Membership of the board is proportional to membership of the federations (Cosatu has 19 affiliates with 1.8 million members; Fedusa has 27 affiliates, with half a million members. Ditsela 1998a, p.6)

sending its members on Ditsela courses.[12] Cosatu representatives, too, have suggested that Ditsela should concentrate on skills development, and leave political education to the federation's own education department or to its affiliates.

It has been argued elsewhere (Cooper, 1997a) that in South Africa's new democracy the distinct political and ideological identity of the radical labour education tradition that challenged apartheid has been giving way to the blurring of boundaries between labour education on the one hand, and workplace training and education on the part of employers on the other. Given this, one of Ditsela's key challenges is to rebuild the working class identity of labour education in South Africa – while at the same time confronting issues of diversity within the working class.

Maintaining a collective approach in the face of increasing individualism

Since the early 1990s, the labour movement has been a driving force in the area of national policy development on workplace education and training, and has played a key role in the establishment of a new National Qualifications Framework (NQF), which, it argued, would provide workers with access to training and redress for their historical exclusion from educational opportunities. It could be argued that the very formation of Ditsela was illustrative of a parallel process happening within the trade union movement towards the institutionalization, formalization and professionalization of labour education. Since its establishment, Ditsela has been under consistent and growing pressure to seek formal accreditation of its courses, and more recently, to get involved in the training of trade unionists around workplace training issues.

The pressure towards formal accreditation has been expressed both directly and indirectly. During Ditsela's first Educator Conference in 1997, worker delegates expressed strong support for formal certification of worker education. Since then, this view has been echoed in numerous Ditsela research reports. An investigation into the changing role of trade union organizers reported that "All interviewees unanimously said that formal accreditation of trade union education will uplift the status of the education, 'open doors for further learning' and will also enhance organizer's career paths."[13] Individual quotes from organizers demonstrate how South Africa trade unionists today are strongly influenced by aspirations towards individual upward mobility:

> The skills you acquire in the trade union movement are enormous and the lack of formal accreditation stifles your mobility...

---

[12] Fedusa participation has been much lower that than of Cosatu, even taking account of its much smaller membership, and its level of participation has dropped over time.

[13] These views are also echoed in Ditsela's 1997 report on 'the competencies of trade union educators' (Ditsela 1997d, p.6).

Formal accreditation will also change the image of organizers from being instigators of trouble to being respectable members of society… (Ditsela 2000b, p.20).

Two consecutive Ditsela research reports (1997a; 1998b) profiling trade union education capacity found that more than half of all Cosatu officials were engaged in private study, most often in formal education institutions, and that their motivation was to make themselves more "marketable" outside the union. (Ditsela, 1998d; Bughlungu, 2000). Samson argues that: "The trends show that for many unionists, unions have become stepping stones to the corporate world and the government" (Ditsela, 1998d, p.13).

There have been some heated debates within the labour movement around the formalization and accreditation of trade union education, with some strong opposition to this process also being expressed. Those opposing formalization and accreditation argue that labour education is essentially collective in nature, and that accreditation will individualize trade union education and take away its political thrust (Ditsela, 1997e; Cooper, 1997b;1998b).

The pressure on Ditsela to move into the role of offering "marketable qualifications" to trade unionists has been intensified by a process of outside providers – universities, a mushrooming sector of private colleges, as well as employers –moving in to compete aggressively for a new "adult education" market, *including* a "trade unionist" market. As early as 1997, Ditsela noted that both management and consultants were playing an increasing role in shop-steward training, while unions found it difficult to get shop-stewards to their own courses: "either shop stewards see no need to attend or management refuses time off" (Ditsela, 1997c, p.14). The 1997 SWOP survey found Fedusa affiliates making extensive use of universities and "technikon" for union-related education. A 2000 Ditsela report notes:

A worrying development is that some unions are engaging the services of private consultants/institutions …. that do not have either a proven record of delivery, sympathy or understanding of trade union concerns, and who appear to be ready to exploit the fact that they can provide some form of accreditation (Ditsela, 2000a, p.8).

Labour has thus become a lucrative new market for the new education and training industry in South Africa.

Ditsela has noted these developments with concern:

These trends appear to de-value trade union (including Ditsela) provision (and) it also means that trade unionists are increasingly upgrading their skills and knowledge in courses that have little affinity to trade union principles and values – and may, indeed, even be biased against trade unions and the working class.

Other concerns are that while Ditsela has been given the role of developing a trade union approach to formal accreditation, trade union federations and their affiliates lack any clear, co-ordinated policy on these issues. A Ditsela report concludes that this is, in turn, linked to "… a lack of a common approach to trade union education – including its purpose, principles and the politics of trade union education." (Ditsela, 2000c)

In 2000, the Ditsela Board made a formal decision that Ditsela should seek formal accreditation of some of its courses and should lead a process of developing a qualification structure for trade union staff. This process is now underway, but it is clear from the frequent reservations that have been expressed in Ditsela documents that it is a process tht enjoys only qualified support. For example:

- Union education must not become too academic. There must be political intentions for defending the working class

- Standard setting and accreditation cannot be a technical exercise divorced from the strategic direction of the labour movement

- The identity of Ditsela and trade union education is critical and should be held on to. Courses cannot be "handed over" to universities (Ditsela, 1998 May Board Meeting; Ditsela 2000b: p.23-24).

Since its inception, the issue of formal accreditation of its courses has seemed to be inescapable for Ditsela. Some see the process of accreditation of trade union education and the development of a qualification structure for trade union employees as an opportunity to bring greater coherence and quality to labour education. Others not only have serious political reservations about this prospect, but fear that labour educators will drown in the sea of bureaucratic red tape that is likely to emerge with the institution of formal assessment.

Ditsela: Mirroring the fault-lines of the South African labour movement?

It is not possible to give an adequate assessment of the challenges facing labour education generally, or Ditsela in particular, outside of a broader analysis of the serious issues facing the South Africa labour movement more generally.

During 1980s, the non-racial trade union movement was arguably the single most important organized force of internal political resistance. During the '90s however, the union movement was weakened by several factors. It lost membership through massive retrenchments, particularly in mining and manufacturing. At the same time, it expanded into other sectors, significantly amongst public sector workers, including teachers, other professionals and members of the public service. This has led to a change in the composition of its membership, away from its 1980s core of semi-skilled/unskilled black workers, towards a greater number of more formally educated and white-collar workers (Baskin, 1996).

These demographic changes have been accompanied by other problems. The increasing shift towards the decentralization of industrial relations (through out-sourcing, sub-contracting, privatization, and other non-standard

forms of employment) and the growing individualism in the employment relationship make workers far more difficult to organize. Ditsela's research report
The Changing Trade Union Organiser found that organizers are grappling to perform their duties in a changing environment, and that "…workers no longer
use the unions as political outlets but they join them to address their immediate bread and butter issues." Retrenchments and new issues related to
globalization "… have made the workplace very uncertain and have created
high levels of distrust between workers and organizers" (Ditsela, 2000b, p.22).
A leading Cosatu trade unionist has argued that globalization has undermined
collective identities: while capital had "gone global," labour responses to current challenges are like a "series of unconnected nodes of struggle, faced with a
connected economic network" (Ebrahim Patel, quoted in Daniels, 2000, p.8).

These problems, added to a growing number of organizational weaknesses
and a decline in the participatory, democratic culture that characterized the
independent trade union movement in the 1980s, has led to a weakening of
labour's voice, and its growing marginalization within the tripartite political
alliance (Buhlungu, 2000). This has been evident in the ANC's adoption of
GEAR (Growth, Employment and Redistribution strategy), an economic policy representing a shift away from its earlier redistributive vision towards the
ideology of the free market, and more recently by proposed new legislation
which threatens to withdraw some of the rights won by workers after 1994.

The ambiguous relationship between Cosatu and the ANC government
has attracted criticism both from within and without the federation. A
well-known labour commentator, writing after Cosatu's national congress in
September 2000, argued that Cosatu could be in danger of becoming an
example of "skorokoro" unionism – described by the September Commission[14] as a form of unionism which "zigzags from problem to problem." He
argues that there is a fundamental contradiction between its professed goal of
socialism and an emerging trend of business unionism, and between its con-
demnation of the shift of the ANC to the right, while continuing to reaffirm its
support for the ANC government. He also points to an "emerging culture of
political silencing" which stifles debate and discourages serious analysis of
weaknesses and challenges (Buhlungu, 2000).

Against this background, it is not surprising that labour education organizations such as Ditsela face such a daunting task to rebuild a weakened and
fragmented system of labour education. It is not surprising that Ditsela is
under pressure – in a growing context of individualism – to develop career
paths for trade unionists, and that it struggles to find clear political answers to
how to deal with such pressures while still seeking to assert a clear, working
class identity for labour education.

---

[14] An important Cosatu commission, set up under the chairpersonship of Connie September in 1997, to make
recommendations on the future organizational shape and political direction of Cosatu.

Future challenges

It has been shown here that many of the challenges facing labour educators in South Africa are unique to the particular history and context of worker organization and workers' struggles in this country. However, there are other challenges that seem to be more universal in nature and are products of South Africa being part of a globalizing society increasingly dominated by the commodification of information and knowledge.

Today in South Africa, in a context where national education policy is based on "consensus politics" that assumes the essential compatibility of all "stakeholder interests," a key challenge facing labour educators is to re-assert the working class identity of labour education, and to re-shape it to meet the challenges facing the workers' movement in a new South Africa. They will need to decide how, and to what extent, they engage with the burgeoning, competitive "workplace training industry," and whether it is possible to do so while at the same time asserting the value of trade union education. Labour educators will also need to find ways to challenge capitalist notions of skills and productivity and re-assert the possibility that workers' skills and knowledge can be put to collective, social use rather than simply serving the interests of profitability and international competitiveness. Rebuilding the value and identity of worker education in South Africa will also require the successful development of a unified approach to labour education out of very diverse political traditions, and perhaps even more importantly, the development of an approach that will unify workers in a context of the deepening erosion of collectivities and traditions of solidarity.

Labour educators generally in South Africa, and organizations such as Ditsela in particular, will also need to make some critical choices. They will have to decide whether they build a system of labour education that is responsive primarily to those workers who are best organized and most articulate, or whether (directly or indirectly) they can also make a difference to those workers who are most exploited, have the fewest rights, and who are least "educated" – for example, farmworkers isolated on (still) white-owned farms; those workers who eke a living out of irregular bouts of employment in poor, rural towns; or the hundreds and thousands of domestic workers who work (mainly but not exclusively) in "white" kitchens. Labour educators will also need to choose whether they put all their energy and resources into the development of a formalized *system* of trade union education, or whether their work will also be shaped by workers' experiences of informal learning and knowledge production that are far wider, richer and deeper than those that can take place within organized classrooms and programs.

Note: Although the author sits as an education advisor on the governing board of Ditsela this chapter is written in a personal capacity. She is grateful to Ditsela for allowing access to its documents and is indebted to a large number of trade unionists and worker educators for many of the insights and understandings expressed.

REFERENCES

* *Ditsela documents:*

  * Ditsela (1997a). A Trade Union Educational Needs and Capacity Assessment: Phase One Report: Head Office Survey; Prepared by Sociology of Work Unity (SWOP), University of Witwatersrand, July.
  * Ditsela (1997b). Building a Workers Education Movement: Ditsela Educators Conference, Johannesburg 30 July – 2 August: Draft Report on the Proceedings.
  * Ditsela (1997c). Pathways, September.
  * Ditsela. (1997d). Board Planning Workshop Documents, 16th October.
  * Ditsela (1997e). Research Report on the Competencies of Trade Union Educators, Prepared for Ditsela and ETDP by Funamna Mankaye, December.
  * Ditsela (1998a). Annual Report, November 1996 – February 1998.
  * Ditsela (1998b). A trade Union Educational Needs and Capacity Assessment: Report on the Phase Two Regional Survey, Draft 2, March.
  * Ditsela (1998c). Ditsela Board Workshop Documents, 11 – 12 June.
  * Ditsela (1998d). Union Education – What Role for the Regions? A Discussion Document by Melanie Samson, August.
  * Ditsela (1998e). Building a Worker Education Movement: Ditsela Progress Report, Educator Conference, 16 – 19 September, Johannesburg.
  * Ditsela (1998f). Building a Worker Education Movement: A First Assessment, Educator Conference: 16 – 19 September, Johannesburg.
  * Ditsela (1999). Pathways, September.
  * Ditsela (2000a). Board Meeting Documents, 24th February.
  * Ditsela (2000b) The changing trade union organiser, A Ditsela Research Report, January – March
  * Ditsela (2000c). Board Planning Workshop documents, 20 – 21 July.
  * Ditsela, Minutes of Board Meetings (1997 – 2000).

* Baskin, J. (ed.) (1996). *Unions in transition: Cosatu at the dawn of democracy.* Johannesburg: NALEDI.
* Buhlungu S. (2000). Unions chart their course in a tough new world. *Sunday Times,* September 10.
* Cooper, L. (1997a). New education policy directions in South Africa: Shifting the boundaries of worker education. Paper presented to 27th Annual SCUTREA Conference, University of London, 1 – 3 July.
* Cooper, L. (1998a). From rolling mass action to 'RPL': The changing discourse of experience and learning in the South African labour movement. *Studies in Continuing Education,* Vol. 20, No 2.
* Daniels, G. (2000). A new role for labour: Unions face new challenges from globalization. *Mail and Guardian Supplement: Work to Rule.* September 22 – 28.
* Davies, R., O'Meara, D. & Dlamini, S. (1984). *The Struggle for South Africa: A Reference Guide to Movements, Organizations and Institutions,* Vol. 1. London: Zed Press.

4

Education for Labour's Professionals: Britain, Canada and the USA

TOM NESBIT

Unions' position within the economy and their involvement with industrial and social change has a notable effect on working and social conditions. Crucial to this end is the cadre of full-time officials and staff who act as the union movement's key administrators, managers, and organizers. The most extensive studies of this cadre's work (Clegg, Killick, & Adams, 1961; Kelly & Heery, 1994; Mills, 1948; Watson, 1988) indicate that union officials have an ever-widening range of responsibilities which fall mainly into three broad functions: servicing and representing union members, organizing and recruiting new members, and representing and promoting the policies of the union. In addition, they are often expected to "provide the integrative and inspirational leadership which will harmonize the interests of ethnically and occupationally divergent members and build solidarity towards common goals" (Gray, 1975, pp. 472-473).

Union officials are also expected to keep up with technological, economic and legislative changes. For example, recent developments in computer and office technology have necessitated changes in officials' working practices. In addition, their work is often significantly affected by legislative changes and the transformations in industry and employment brought about by economic globalization (Brecher, Costello, & Smith, 2000; Turner, 1991). These changes have tended to aggravate an already excessive workload to the extent that many officials experience a significant amount of physical and emotional stress. As a recent study of union staff workload indicates, "many union representatives and office workers are at risk of burning out trying to meet heavy job demands" (Lowe, 1998, p. 250).

Union officials have sometimes been described as the labour movement's professionals, equivalent to professional workers in other spheres (Kelly & Heery, 1994). As dominant definitions of professionalism usually depend upon the possession of unique forms of expertise often acquired through formal education and training (Eraut, 1994), one might expect labour organizations to have developed systems of training and professional development for their own officials and staff. However, as a 1975 US study found, "union leadership is perhaps the only major profession...for which there is no established and recognized sequence of professional training" (Gray, 1975, p. 472). In 1991, Clark and Gray described the training of union officials as "an ad hoc, unsystematic process at best" (p. 191), and Eaton (1995) found that many US labour leaders predominantly acquired their leadership skills by the "sink or swim" approach. Further, Kelly and Heery's (1994) study of British trade unions found only a few unions that "develop a strategic approach to training, in which there is an attempt to specify the objectives of training policy, identify officers' training needs, and provide a system of release and cover for officers involved in training" (p. 62). Although some steps have been recently taken in Britain and the USA to remedy this, most union officials appear "to learn by doing, without much help or encouragement from anyone, and without formal training" (Eaton, 1995, p. 17).

Related Literature

The forms and functions of labour education are already well documented (e.g., Dwyer, 1977; Holford, 1994; Newman, 1993; Rogin & Rachlin, 1968; Spencer, 1994). These studies discuss the general provision of labour education, its goals and approaches, and related values and ideologies. However, such studies rarely examine, in any detail, the different types of education and training provided for different levels within union organizations. Ironically, although labour movements worldwide conduct extensive training for their members and officials and regularly monitor and evaluate their provision, reports are rarely published. Indeed, only in the USA (Allen, 1962; Gray, 1975; Kerrison & Levine, 1960) and Britain (Brown & Lawson, 1972; Fisher & Holland, 1990; Trades Union Congress, 1972) does research focus specifically on the education and training of labour's professionals.

These studies reveal a relative paucity of such training. Rather than receiving preparation for their job through formal education, most union staff and officials still appear to acquire the necessary expertise and attributes through some form of lay apprenticeship where commitment to the union and a proven record of relevant industrial experience count far more than any formal or professional qualifications (Fisher & Holland, 1990). New full-time officials have usually served several years as lay activists acquiring negotiating and public speaking skills as well as a detailed knowledge of the union's constitution, rules, administrative procedures, and the consultative and bargaining machinery. Although some unions require prospective officials to pass an examination, there is "no generally-accepted corpus of theoretical or practical knowledge, no standard training for entrants, and no professional qualification for trade union work" (Kelly & Heery, p. 61). In addressing this situation, a review of the approaches adopted in Great Britain, the USA, and Canada will highlight various options.

Great Britain

British unions expect their officials, after appointment, to supplement their expertise with additional training. A 1991 Trades Union Congress (TUC) survey showed that almost two-fifths of Britain's unions had sent at least 25% of their officers on training courses in the previous year and more than 50% in the previous five years. Much of this training was provided by the TUC itself via an extensive series of national and regional short courses. Most recently, the TUC has been involved in the development of National Vocational Qualifications – occupational standards – for union full-time officials (TUC, 1993). In essence, these standards detail what officers need to know in order to carry out their jobs (see Figure 1).

As the TUC freely admits, these standards are not intended to be read as a comprehensive shopping list of tasks: they only describe the outcomes or the intended results of activities. Also, they only describe outcomes that are the responsibility, or in the control, of individual officials; there may be other complicating factors outside of individual control. The TUC intends its standards to help unions and their staff make a more informed "assessment of their own training and personal development needs or they can be used in a more formal system of training needs analysis" (1993, p. 13). The future use of these standards in labour education seems guaranteed, particularly as the TUC is considering expanding the project to also cover lay and other voluntary officials. Finally, although the standards and the associated National Vocational Qualifications have been heavily endorsed by unions, what's uncertain is the degree to which they have been accepted by officials themselves. The TUC has yet to publish any results; anecdotal evidence suggests that few officials have catalogued the achievements necessary for the NVQ award of competence.

USA

The US labour movement has long recognized the necessity of formal training for union leaders. In the 1920s and 1930s a number of residential schools were set up to train union activists; the most notable were Brookwood Labor College in New York, Highlander in Tennessee, and Bryn Mawr College in Pennsylvania (Clark & Gray, 1991). Now, union officials who require training either attend their own union's residential centres (e.g., the United Auto Workers' Michigan site or that of the International Association of Machinists in Maryland) or go to labour studies programs arranged through a local college or university: more than 50 post-secondary institutions in 30 states currently list some form of labour studies program.

One of the oldest examples of this type is Harvard University's Trade Union Program, which yearly provides an intensive 10-week program for approximately 30 experienced union officials and senior staff away from the day-to-day pressure of work. The success of this program has encouraged

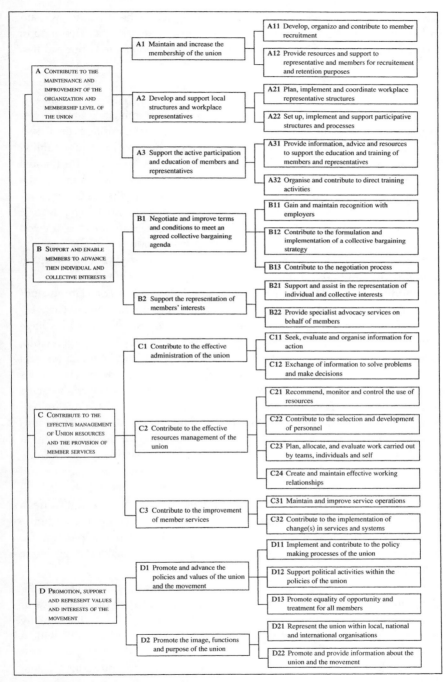

Figure 1: Functional Map to Unit of Competence.

other universities to develop similar programs – such as the graduate program in Labor Studies at the University of Massachusetts at Amherst. Designed in conjunction with the AFL/CIO's George Meany Center for Labor Studies, this program also emphasizes union leadership and administration.

Canada

Canadian unions usually eschew partnerships with universities and prefer to educate and train their own staff and officials – as, for example, at the Canadian Auto Workers' centre at Port Elgin, Ontario. The most extensive training provision occurs at the Canadian Labour Congress's five-week Residential Program, delivered in two parts: a national four-week component at the Labour College of Canada plus an extra week in one of the CLC's regions. Consisting of five courses – economics, political science, sociology, history, and law, each with a specific focus on labour – the program aims "to develop leadership by increasing the ability of unionists to understand, analyze, and deal with everyday problems and issues that may confront them at work, in their unions, and in the community" (1999 Program brochure, p. 2).

In addition, several Canadian universities offer some form of a labour studies certificate or degree program. However, they are not targeted exclusively to union officials and staff. Nevertheless, several recent collaborations have attempted to design educational programs specifically for labour leadership. In the past five years, Simon Fraser University in British Columbia has run two successful nine-month certificate programs for senior provincial labour leaders. Designed in partnership with the Canadian Labour Congress's Pacific Region and the BC Federation of Labour, the programs aimed to develop participants' understanding of a range of labour management issues while also broadening their awareness of practical tools available for the efficient management and leadership of unions. Core courses – leadership, economics, union administration, union as employer, and strategic management and planning – address the specific needs of trade union leaders. Athabasca University in Alberta and the CLC's Labour College of Canada also jointly offer a university-level distance learning course which can be taken either by home study (correspondence) or online via the Internet. It is both a preparation for the residential program of the College and an introduction to the academic field of labour studies.

Although alternatives exist for unions to train their full-time staff and officials, what's uncertain is how many take advantage of such opportunities or what factors have an impact on such training. A recent study that directly explored these issues found that although most unions in Canada provide a wealth of resources for shop steward and other lay official training, there was markedly less support for those in permanent or full-time positions (Nesbit, 2000). As most unions expect their staff and officials to be competent to perform their jobs when hired, extra training is generally considered unnecessary.

If further training was considered appropriate, many unions claimed to encourage new officials to attend existing labour education courses. However, none of these programs is regarded as being specifically geared for the particular needs of full-time officials: "[lay representatives] are the folks who need it most," claimed a CLC staff member. "We expect the full-timers to either know the stuff already or catch up as best they can." Additionally, most lay official courses are heavily focused on skills development rather than on developing the broader understanding necessary for full-time staff: "they're more job training than labour studies," as one national representative put it.

Discussion and implications

Clearly, there are problems associated with developing education and training in unions that are part organization, part social movement. Those who work full-time for unions tend, and are also generally encouraged, to view their needs and interests as secondary to the demands of the membership. Despite this, several union leaders expressed grave concern about the amount of training provided for full-time officials. As the president of one of Canada's major unions put it:

> You get elected to a full-time national position and suddenly you're a manager. And when people elect you the last thing they're thinking is whether you have good management skills. So, things like time management, organizing your own work or organizing other people's work...they become major issues.

The same issues were also identified at a regional level. "When our folks get elected to regional positions they have to learn a whole new set of skills – they have different responsibilities and different concerns and there are different issues," said one regional coordinator. "Really, we don't help them much. So, for the first year they flounder a bit ... after that they generally get the hang of it...but it can sometimes cost us."

Despite these sentiments, there appeared to be little concerted effort to develop systematic training for labour's professionals. Yet most senior union officials have participated in, and recognize, labour education's crucial role in the building of the labour movement. What might explain this disparity?

There appear to be both personal and structural influences on the provision of education for union officials. One is the tension between an individual need and the efforts required to support a collective organization. "I'd feel so guilty taking time off," was one official's comment. "I know I'd benefit from more training but the members' problems must come first." Related to this sentiment is the individual nature of most union work. As one official explained, "Much of my time is spent developing working relationships, whether with the members or with employers. That's my responsibility...and I can't just leave that...if I want to go on a course." Most officials indicated that they had little time for attending education programs and that their education was best advanced by attending local and national conferences. In short, training is perceived as an individual responsibility and expected to be incorporated into existing work schedules.

Officials are often ambivalent towards education: "People forget that union education is not just about raising individual awareness or increasing a person's knowledge; it's more seeing those goals in a more collective setting." There is also a concern that courses might be too inappropriate or too academic. "The last thing the union movement needs is an MBA," was a typical response.

Several organizational factors also affect the provision of education. The first is a union's size. Briefly, small unions have far fewer resources in general and allocate much less towards labour education. "If you've got a region with only 12 officials and they're spread out across four provinces and two islands...freeing a couple of people up to go on a course is going to be quite difficult." The cost too can be prohibitive: "the amount of money we spend flying people around is enormous."

A second factor involves a union's priorities. Often education has to take second place to a union's other functions such as organizing, servicing members, or negotiating contracts. Because these latter activities are generally the more visible aspects of a union's work (and hence, where members judge union effectiveness), they receive greater prominence. Significantly, few unions allocate any specific resources, develop training policies, or operate any system of performance appraisal – a common way of identifying training needs in other organizations.

A third, powerful influence might be best described as relating to a union's organizational culture (Tuomisto, 1993). The relationships between union culture and education are complex. D'Arcy Martin (1995) speaks of the dynamics or "cross-currents" of union culture which can help identify the supports and barriers for education within unions themselves and the movement generally. One key dynamic – what Martin names the "oppressive/affirmative" – is the presence in unions of inequalities and hierarchies of power. Women officials, for example, are often a significant presence at a local level yet are far less likely to hold a more senior or national post. One senior woman official described her first year as a national official:

> It was dreadful...I was running around all over the country, never too sure of what I was doing or where I was going next. I never knew when I'd be home. I felt permanently exhausted. I know other women feel the same...there's got to be a better way of doing it than this.

The selection of officials for further education can itself be political: "Sometimes, whom the president chooses to send is quite contentious. If you're in favour, you get to go."

Another dynamic – "servicing/mobilizing" – is the ever-present need for unions to provide immediate practical help while also creating a climate for broader social transformation around issues such as social justice and human rights. This dynamic is often dichotomized into "business" versus "social" unionism – and unions do tend to adopt one approach over the other. However, Martin's point is that, regardless of approach, such a tension is present in every union activity. Busy officials, ever responsive to the demands of the membership, can always find reasons not to make time for reflection or planning. Yet the opportunity to engage in these activities is precisely what many officials claim they value from education courses. As one senior official who had traveled widely put it,

> My experience having looked at a variety of unions in a variety of countries is that the ones that take a more proactive approach to education and make time for more strategic planning are the ones that can best deal with the problems of globalization.

These dynamics highlight the role that unions can play in implementing a culture of learning at work – not least in their own working environments. Unions everywhere want their members to acquire and improve the skills, knowledge, and qualifications that enhance their employability and increase earnings, autonomy, and self-esteem. They regularly bargain over workplace training and develop training partnerships and strategies with employers and governments. As Sarah Perman (TUC Spokesperson) puts it, "unions have long recognized that...companies that invest in training and development are best placed to deal with the challenges of new technology, global trade, and industrial change" (1998, p. 26). What better way for unions to underscore this recognition than by implementing training initiatives within their own organizations?

One of the chief measures of labour education – including that provided for officials and staff – is how far it strengthens labour organization. From this standpoint, a union's internal organization might be strengthened through expanding educational provision. For example, training can help unions explore their own internal practices and how they might generate resentment and alienation. While discussing union culture, two senior women officials (from different unions) identified a discrepancy between labour's progressive rhetoric and conservative practices. For them, this tendency could often be seen in union education programs that "privileged technical skills rather than fostered imagination or provided support." Susan Eaton's (1995) study of women in trade union leadership also noted this tendency. She suggests that all women, especially minority women, request training programs more often than men. So, as one of the recommendations of the CLC women's report states, "unions, as employers, should develop more pro-active staff training programs" (1998, p. 2). The report quotes one long time union activist:

A critical analysis and discussion of power, self-interest, and decision-making must happen within our own organizations as well. This is essential for all of us – staff, leaders, and members. When organizational structures are hidden or not discussed, people are disempowered. When our own organizational structures are not easily understood, people learn that they have to be "in with the in crowd" to be involved in the union. This is one of the common ways that sexism, racism, and stagnation prevail in many organizations. (Conrow, 1991, p. 51)

Conclusion

Trade unions have always been faced with the necessity of adjusting to economic, technological, labour market, legislative and public attitudinal changes. Yet as the current pace of change is accelerating, the demands to modify union structures and policies to accommodate and resist such challenges are growing. Globalization may appear the most pressing challenge, but addressing it necessarily invokes looking at unions themselves (Mantsios, 1998). Yet unions do not always find it easy to take up the challenge of critically examining their own practices. Despite the presence of some remarkably thoughtful and far-sighted leaders in union movements worldwide, the pressures of work allow little time for reflection or strategic analysis. In addition, the reactive nature of much of union activity combines with their inherent insularity and traditionalism to hinder education or training that might question these tendencies.

One of a union's greatest assets is its personnel: those dedicated and hard-working staff and officials who perform the often-mundane tasks of running the organization whilst also keeping its spirit alive. Union leaders today act as much as administrators and analysts as they do as bargainers or spokespersons, and, as such, require training and support for those roles. In 1970, a study claimed that leadership training was one of the principal challenges facing the US union movement. As the authors then stated,

> society has already entered a world in which common sense and general intelligence are no longer sufficient to solve most problems facing large, complex organizations ….Unions will find themselves at a disadvantage in dealing with organizations which have the needed information and trained talent (Bok & Dunlop, 1970, p. 469).

Thirty years on, as the problems facing unions and their leaders seem so much greater, so do the opportunities.

___

Author's Note: This chapter is based on research conducted by the author and Carla Lipsig-Mummé (York University) and funded by the Social Sciences and Humanities Research Council of Canada. A full report of the study is available either from the author or from the Centre for Research on Work & Society at York University.

REFERENCES

- Allen, R. (1962). The professional in unions and his educational preparation. *Industrial and Labor Relations Review, 16* (1), 16-29.

- Bok, D., & Dunlop, J. T. (1970). *Labor and the American community.* New York: Simon & Schuster.

- Brecher, J, Costello, T, & Smith, B. (2000). *Globalization from below.* Cambridge, MA: South End Press.

- Brown, W., & Lawson, M. (1972). *The training of trade union officers.* Coventry, UK: University of Warwick, Industrial Relations Research Unit.

- Canadian Labour Congress. (1998). *Feminist organizing models.* Women's symposium, November 1-3, 1998.

- Clark, P. F., & Gray, L. S. (1991). Union administration. In G. Strauss, D. G. Gallagher, & J. Fiorito (Eds.), *The state of the unions,* (pp. 175-200). Madison, WI: Industrial Relations Research Association.

- Clegg, H. A., Killick, A., & Adams, R. (1961). *Trade union officers.* Oxford: Blackwell.

- Conrow, T. (1991). Contract servicing from an organizing model: Don't bureaucratize, organize. *Labour Research Review,* 17, 45-59.

- Dwyer, R. (1977). Workers' education, labor education, labor studies: An historic delineation. *Review of Educational Research, 47,* 179-207.

- Eaton, S. C. (1995). Union leadership development in the 1990s and beyond. *Workplace Topics, 4* (2).

- Eraut, M. (1994). *Developing professional knowledge and competence.* London: Falmer Press.

- Fisher J., & Holland, D. (1990). *Training for full-time officers of trade unions.* London: Further Education Unit.

- Gray, L. S. (1975). Training of labor union officials. *Labor Law Journal,* August, 472-477.

- Holford, J. (1994). *Union education in Britain: A TUC activity.* Nottingham, UK : Department of Adult Education, University of Nottingham.

- Kelly, J., & Heery, E. (1994). *Working for the union.* Cambridge: Cambridge University Press.

- Kerrison, I. L. H., & Levine. H. A. (1960). *Labor leadership education.* New Brunswick, NJ: Rutgers University Press.

- Lowe, G. S. (1998). The future of work: Implications for unions. *Relations Industrielles/Industrial Relations, 53* (2), 235-257.

- Mantsios, G. (Ed.). (1998). *A new labor movement for a new century.* New York: Monthly Review Press.

- Martin, D'A. (1995). *Thinking union.* Toronto: Between the Lines Press.

- Mills, C. Wright. (1950). *The new men of power.* New York: Harcourt Brace.

- Nesbit, T. (2000). Training labour's professionals. Paper presented at the 4th Annual Conference of the Labour Education & Training Research Network, October 22-24, Vancouver, Canada.

- Newman, M. (1993). *The third contract: Theory and practice in trade union training.* Paddington, Australia: Stewart Victor Publishing.

- Perman, S. (1998). The learning age. *Adults Learning,* April 1998, 26-27.

- Rogin, L., & Rachlin, M. (1968). *Labor education in the United States.* Washington, DC: National Institute of Labor Education at The American University.

* Spencer, B. (1994). Educating union Canada. *Canadian Journal for the Study of Adult Education, 8* (2), 45-64.

* Trades Union Congress. (1972). *Training full-time officers.* London: Author.

* Trades Union Congress (1993). *Trade union standards and qualifications.* London: Author

* Tuomisto, J. (1993). *A cultural perspective on the study of trade union education.* Paper presented at ESREA conference on Popular Adult Education and Social Mobilization in Europe. Linköping, Sweden, August 7-10, 1993.

* Turner, L. (1991). *Democracy at work: Changing world markets and the future of labor unions.* Ithaca, NY: Cornell University Press.

* Watson, D. (1988). *Managers of discontent: Trade union officials and industrial relations managers.* London: Routledge.

5

A Chinese Perpsective on Workers' Rights in Labour Education

RITA KWOK HOI YEE

My friends in Western countries make an assumption that one aim of labour education is to promote workers' rights. Of course, we share a commitment to end the oppression of workers, and to empower people through participatory learning. However, from my experience and research in Hong Kong and China, I have found the idea of rights very complicated culturally, and the identity of "worker" conditioned by people's historical experience. This chapter reflects on the concepts of rights among workers in China, issues of worker identity and the implications for educational practice.

Concepts of rights

When I talk with labour educators from other countries, we usually consider four types of rights: Civil rights refer to the legal relationship between individuals and the state: these rights protect citizens against the abuse of power from state authorities. Political rights relate to participation in public affairs, including the choice of government through elections and voting. Social rights are entitlements for which citizens hold the state responsible, such as health care and education. Finally, economic rights refer to entitlements to income, particularly fair wages.

These four types of rights appear in a distinct way in the Chinese literature on rights (Xia, 1992; You, 1994; Zhu, 1995). Two strands of philosophical thought, namely, traditional Chinese Confucian values and Marxism, have been major historical contributors in shaping Chinese concepts of rights. More recently, the Western liberal approach may have gained some prominence as a consequence of China's shift to a market economy. The combination of these three traditions is a basis for assessing the potential for independent worker organizations emerging in China, and creating space for labour education of the sort now widespread in Western societies.

Confucian concepts and the notion of rights

The Confucian philosophy does not encompass an explicit theory of rights, as the notion of rights itself never existed in the traditional Chinese culture. (Xia, 1992; King,1993; Hansen, 1994; De Bary and Tu, 1998). Nevertheless, democratic elements that constitute the modern notions of rights, such as humanism and equality, are not unfamiliar in the classical writings of the Confucian school. Yet the significance attached to these components could never be comparable to the idea of harmony, the foundation of Confucian teaching on which other doctrines are built. According to Li Chi (The Book of Rites), Confucius's ideal society, namely the "Society of Great Similarity," which represents the highest stage of civilization, is a society of perfect social equality and harmony (Hsu, 1975, p. 237). Thus, harmony is the ultimate goal and the guiding principle of social relations in Chinese society. Moreover, as the State (government) is seen as a part of social life, achieving harmony has in fact become a determining criterion of good governance.

In the above context, a Western idea of individual worker rights simply makes no sense. Chinese traditions reject the liberal notion of an abstract and isolated individual. The suppression of the individual self mainly rests on two sources, the "ownership" relation between parent and child, and the dominance of social community.

Traditional Chinese culture is characterized by the primacy of community over the individual, as the individual is not treated as a separate entity but as part of an organic whole, part of a family or clan in particular. The self is equivalent to a person's social role and one's social relation with others, such as ruler-subject, father-son, husband-wife, brothers and friends. "There can be no me in isolation, to be considered abstractly. I am the totality of roles. I live in relation to specific others. I do not play or perform these roles. I am these roles." (Rosemont, 1988, p.177, quoted by Hansen, 1994, p.1). Thus the concept of inherent, individual human dignity embedded in the Western concept of natural rights is alien to traditional Chinese values.

A Chinese scholar, Xia Yong, affirms that the major difference between the Chinese concept of rights and those of Western culture is rooted in the definition of justice. Justice as defined in Western societies maintains "a balance between rights and obligation," while in Chinese society "justice is fulfilling one's obligation" (Xia, 1992). In a society where collective interest is emphasized over interest of individuals, claiming one's rights is considered selfish and egocentric, while sacrificing one's rights (entitlements) for the good of the community is considered an act of justice. Imagine in this context a labour education practice based on claiming rights against the collective.

Marx and Maoist conception of rights

Five thousand years of traditional Confucian thinking was challenged during the 50 years of Maoist leadership. A compromise of Marxism was the interesting outcome. In Marxist thought, the goal of human rights is the emancipation of the human being, not attainable in a class-based capitalist society. Bourgeois rights are limited, as "right can never be higher than the economic structure of society and its cultural development" (Marx, Critique of the Gotha

Program, 1875). Thus bourgeois rights, having played a positive historical role in overthrowing feudalism, were to be obsolete in communism.

Tou (1993) in his book Confucianism vs. Marxism has identified some common elements between the two ideologies. Confucius and Marx share similar optimism about the power of morality in transforming human nature. Confucius's ideal "Society of Great Similarity" is a society of perfect harmony and equality. Li Chi (Book of Rites) holds that:

> when the great principle of the great similarity prevails, the whole world becomes a republic, possessing a common spirit. The people elect men of talents, virtue, and ability. Their words are sincere, and they cultivate universal harmony. Thus men do not regard as their parents only their own parents, nor treat as their children only their own children. A competent provision is made for the aged until their death, employment for the able bodied, and means of education for the young. ...Each man has his proper work and each woman has her proper home. This sounds surprisingly like Marx, in fact. At this stage, there is no state, and the family ceases to be the foundation of social and political organization, and there is no private property nor inequality of classes (Hsu, 1975, p.239).

Compare this with Marx's utopia, specified in the Critique of the Gotha Program (1875):

> after the servitude of subordination to the division of labour has disappeared, and with it the opposition between mental and physical labour, after labour has become, not only a means of life, but the primary need of life, after each individual's productive power has increased with his all-around development and all the springs of cooperative wealth flow more freely – only then can the narrow limits of bourgeois right be wholly left behind, and can society inscribe upon its banners: from each according his ability, to each according to his needs (Tucker,1978).

Of course, Mao developed his own synthesis of traditional Confucian and Marxist approaches to human rights:

> Human rights belong to the bourgeoisie, and could not be applied to the proletariat; Due to the needs of revolution and class struggle, human rights should not be taken seriously because "human" is only a concept without reference to class differences (Mao only embraced the idea of a class rights, but not the idea of human rights) Even if the people of the nation belong to the right class, they held rights only collectively, not as individuals. In short, according to Mao and the party leadership, China did not need human rights. (Zhu, 1995, p.134).

In his writings, the term *people's rights* is used to distinguish collective rights that people hold as a class from individualist human rights.

Mao's rejection of human rights is expressed clearly in his speech "On the correct handling of contradictions among the people," made on February 27, 1957:

> Our socialist democracy is the broadest kind of democracy, such as is not to be found in any bourgeois state ...But this freedom is freedom under leadership and this democracy is democracy under centralized guidance. ..the unity of democracy and centralism, of freedom and discipline, constitutes our democratic centralism. Under this system, the people enjoy broad democracy and freedom, but at the same time they have to keep within the bounds of socialist discipline (cited by Xin, 1979, p.2).

It is clearly stated in the Constitution of the Peoples Republic of China (PRC) that rights are linked to duties to serve the State, and the subordination of rights to socialism. "Every citizen enjoys the rights and at the same time must perform the duties prescribed by the Constitution and the law" (Art.33). The exercise by citizens of the PRC of their freedoms and rights "may not infringe upon the interests of the state, of society and of the collective" (Art. 51).

To some observers, the 1978 reform of Deng Xianping marked a turning point in the conception of rights, especially for Chinese workers. The policy of separating government administration from the enterprise reflects a tendency to devolve national power to society. Since then, in spite of occasional counter-tendencies, the state has generally tended to decentralize power and loosen its grip in the economic sphere (Zhu, 1995, p.123).

Despite the control imposed on political emancipation, legal reform was given a prominent position in the reform agenda, as it is considered a significant condition to attract foreign trades and investment. However, the emphasis given to legal reform does not mean that China is now under the "rule of law" which implies an independent judicial system and the supremacy of law over the state. The term "Fa Zhi" (legal and governed) used in many policy documents can be translated as "rule of law," or "rule by law" or simply "the legal system." Rule by law simply means using a non-arbitrary system of rules to govern, while "rule of law" is a liberal notion, implying a system of laws that protects a pluralist civil society against the state (Brugger, & Reglar, 1994). Until the present, the judicial system has been subjugated to the rule of the party, and the division of powers is still rejected by the government leaders as irrelevant for a socialist society. Thus the promulgation of a comprehensive Labour Act in 1994 was not able to achieve its intended goal, due to judicial discretion which overrides the rule of law in China.

Implications for educational practice

Two issues need to be tackled before any worker education programs can be successfully implemented in a Chinese society, namely legitimization and trust.

The legitimization issue

As indicated by the previous analysis, cultural factors in Chinese societies as well as the interplay of political and economic forces have inhibited the recognition of Western human rights standards, and consequently increased suppression of union militancy, or rather, union legitimacy. Generally, worker educators find no high regard for their contribution in promoting workers rights. On the contrary, they are often labelled as instigators and their educational program dismissed as subversive attempts to breach social harmony.

In addition to external pressure, the largest obstacle comes from workers' internalization of the overpowering emphasis on communal relationship, to the extent that individual rights are often sacrificed. The following case provides a good example.

A few years ago, while my students were delivering a talk on workers, compensation regulations in a hospital, a worker insisted that he would not sue his boss even though he had all of his five fingers chopped off by a defective machine. Surprisingly, in a guilty voice, he said the accident had already cost his boss a large fortune, since the shipment of the goods was delayed! In addition, he had been repeatedly reassured by the boss that he could keep his job despite the loss of his working capacity. He considered this an act of benevolence and trusted that his boss would take care of him like a father. For him, disrupting the paternalistic relationship would sever his only link of material support. His fellow workers would also consider him selfish if he took legal action against the boss, as the whole factory would suffer from the expensive lawsuit, and this might cost them their jobs. This case may sound extreme, but is not uncommon as an initial reaction to work injuries among workers.

Trust

Another obstacle that discourages workers from participating in rights-based programs is a deep-rooted distrust of the protective function of rights. The cynicism is largely a result of the cumulative effect of workers' own bitter experiences. Nearly all the workers I interviewed in China expressed skepticism or cynicism of the trade union's role in defending their rights. At least two workers mentioned that the chair of their union teams up with the management during a mediation process. An independent union movement is still banned as unlawful, and workers do not consider the state-sponsored union could represent their interests. Neither do they believe that labour laws would be actually enforced.

When I asked workers whether they had heard of the Labour Law of PRC, most of them said they had, and some were required by their enterprises to attend classes to study the law. In fact, huge public education campaigns were launched when the labour law was promulgated in 1994. Few of them believed that the Law could actually protect them, as they did not believe that the law would be seriously enforced. However, they are not really disappointed. In a society where the rule of law never existed and rhetoric slogans have been a part of their daily experience, the limitation of the Labour Law as a protective mechanism is not a surprise. Education about labour rights thus loses its attraction and significance. Workers believe that only "quanxi" –the Chinese word for connections, counts. When problems arise, instead of resorting to a formal grievance process through the unions, the workers think that it is more practical to find the right person with influence to act on their behalf.

In Hong Kong, even though the rule of law is still upheld after the takeover by the PRC in 1997, workers share the same cynicism towards union rights. Despite 200 years of British colonial rule, fundamental union rights, such as collective bargaining and protection against discrimination of union members, have never been extended to Hong Kong citizens. A culture of human rights has never developed. Thus, worker educators encounter the same kind of rejection as their counterparts in Mainland China.

The above discussion explains why some deep reflection is necessary to develop workers' education for the particular cultural and historical context of China. Elsewhere, I have proposed a model of human rights education that suggests that the goals, approaches, contents and the role of the educators are closely linked to the level of human rights development of the given society. In a rather loose sense, three levels of development are identified.

Human rights education

Level 1 (advanced stage)

At this stage, the society recognizes and accepts the obligation to provide its members with the rights and freedoms enshrined in the international covenants by:

- ratification of most of the conventions
- inclusion of human rights in the national constitution
- making of domestic laws for the protections of all members of its society against human rights violations (anti-discriminations codes etc.)
- establishment of independent monitoring mechanisms
- provision of resources for the promotion and protection of human rights
- provision of resources for human rights education (human rights education recognized as a core subject in the curriculum at all levels)

Level 2 (rhetorical stage)

At this stage, the state is still apathetic about its obligations in providing human rights to its members. However, pressure from the international community is able to push the government to recognize international standards nominally. Thus:

- international conventions are ratified selectively and with many reservations
- no corresponding domestic laws exist to safeguard human rights protections
- few or no resources are allocated for human rights education
- citizens are not aware of their rights
- human rights activities are discouraged and censored by the cultivation of anti-rights social norms

Level 3 (suppressed stage)

The society is very hostile towards the assertion of human rights. Fundamental rights and freedoms of its members are systematically violated by:

- institutionalized abuses of power or oppressive domestic laws (counter-revolution crime, I.S.A, Public Order Ordinances etc.)
- suppression of human rights activities and prosecution of human rights activists
- international monitoring rejected as interference in internal affairs
- anti-rights sentiments perpetuated by official propaganda (media, school systems)

At the advanced stage, the goal of human rights education is focused on the improvement of the existing system and guarding against abuses or under-utilization. Another important goal is to ensure the extension of rights to minority or marginalized groups. In other words, human rights education is often recognized as an integral component of civic education, aimed at enhancing its members with the knowledge and capacity to exercise these rights. In societies where human rights are ignored or suppressed, worker education may take on a revolutionary and political stance. The aim of the programs should emphasize the participation and the empowering of the people.

China and Hong Kong are at stages 3 and 2, respectively, of human rights development. The goals and approaches of rights-based workers' education should emphasize more the elimination of injustice within the labour system. Confronted with the prevailing apathetic attitude and cynicism, worker educators must identify the "right" entry point in order to break the culture of silence and to establish a trusting relationship. One option is a crisis-intervention approach, which combines organizing with education. Educators first of all actively approach workers during a crisis, such as a plant closure, or a massive layoff. During the organizing process, transformative Freirean type of study circles may be formed, but usually organizing takes the form of strategic meetings. These informal groups can be quite successful in "conscientizing" workers of their oppressive situations, and helping them to develop strategies collectively to solve their problems.

In the case of Mainland China, it is evident that workers are already fed up with official campaigns. Yet for most workers, it would be risky to take part in activities organized by unofficial workers' groups, and there would be fear of labelling and political reprisal. The conflict between claiming one's rights and feeling selfish must also be tackled. Thus a consciousness-raising process is a prerequisite to "unburden" workers from the guilt of claiming one's rights, and informal groups can provide the flexibility and security that is important in an unsupportive environment.

Conclusion

In Chinese societies as in the West, rights-based workers' education is an important part of the labour movement. This is particularly true in a social context where the notion of individual rights has been institutionally denied as promoting egoism and atomism at the expense of community and harmony (Baynes, 2000). Moreover, the protective function of rights is seriously hampered by political and judicial discretion and educators themselves can be subject to marginalization and political reprisals. In this context, workers' education is a radical activity, requiring careful study of the particular views and conditions of each group of workers.

Author's Note: Thanks to D'Arcy Martin for assistance in writing this chapter.

REFERENCES

- Baynes, K. (2000). Rights as critique and the critique of rights: Karl Marx, Wendy Brown, and the social function of rights. *Political Theory, 28*(4), August 2000, p.451-468
- Brugger, B. & Reglar, S. (1994). *Politics, economy and society in contemporary China.* Stanford, Calif.: Stanford University Press.
- De Bary, W. & Tu, W. (1998). *Confucianism and human rights.* New York: Columbia University Press.
- Henkin, L. (1986). *Chinese philosophy and human rights – an application of comparative ethics.* Hong Kong: University of Hong Kong.
- Hansen, C. (1994). The human rights idea in contemporary China: a comparative perspective. *Human rights in contemporary China.* Taipei: Commerce Press.
- Kwok, R.(1995). Use of simulation games in teaching human rights. *In human rights education pack,* Bangkok: Asian Regional Resource Center for Human Rights Education, 44-88.
- Rosemont, H. (1988). Why take rights seriously? A Confucian critque. In *Human rights and the world's religions* ((pp.167-182). L. S. Rouner. South: University of Notre Dame Press.
- Sullivan, M. J. (1994). The impact of Western political thought in Chinese political discourse on transition from socialism. *World Affairs,* 157.
- Tao, J. (1990). The Chinese moral ethos and the concept of individual rights. *Journal of Applied Philosophy 7*(2), 119-127.
- Tou, T.I. (1993). *Confucianism vs.Marxism* (in Chinese). Lan Zhou: Lan Zhou University Press
- Tucker, R., Ed. (1978). *The Marx-Engels reader.* London: W.W. Norton.
- Waldron, A. (1996, Jan). A regime against its people. *Freedom Review.*
- Xia, Y. (1992). *Ren quan gai nian qi yuan. (The origin of human rights concepts).* Beijing: Chinese University of Politics and Law Press.
- Xin, A. (1979). *China's new democracy.* Hong Kong: Cosmos Books.
- You, H. M. (1994*). Kong zi si xiang ji qi xian dai yi yi (Confucian and its modern meaning).* No place.
- Zhu, F. (1995). Human rights and the political development of contemporary China 1979-1994. In Davis, M., *Human rights and Chinese values: Legal, philosophical and political perspectives.* M. Davis. Hong Kong: Oxford.

UNIT II

LEARNING AT THE LOCAL LEVEL – UNION, WORKPLACE AND COMMUNITY

Kent Wong discusses the work undertaken in organizing immigrant workers in Los Angeles and argues that it illustrates the successful linking of union education to union activity in the community. In particular, the *Justice for Janitors* campaigns have been most impressive and have relied on educational support to bolster activity, recruitment and contract negotiation. As a result, the region around LA has bucked the trend in the US, providing a leading example of union growth.

Although "research circles" (workers conducting their own research into workplace or sector problems) have been around for some time, it is clear from the chapter by Gunilla Härnsten and Lars Holmstrand that this approach has a bright future in strengthening union activity within the union as well as externally. Research circles represent an important alternative for union members wishing to conduct independent "workplace learning" projects, and the authors argue that the method supports participatory democracy within unions and in society.

Chris Holland and Geraldine Castleton provide a comparative chapter on developments in "basic skills" education in the UK and Australia. They argue that unions in both countries need to learn from each other's involvement in state-sponsored schemes if they are to better serve their members' needs. Unions everywhere also need to cement links with sympathetic voluntary agencies and take a lead role in advocacy of language and literacy education if they are to build the union movement along with community activity.

6

Labour Education for Immigrant Workers in the USA

KENT WONG

Immigrant workers played an essential role in building the US labour movement over a century ago. European immigrants from generations past led campaigns to build unions from the garment factories of New York to the coalmines of West Virginia. Today, the US labour movement is experiencing another infusion of immigrant workers within their ranks, this time mainly from Latin America and Asia.

Labour education for immigrant workers must be broadly defined. Immigrant workers are largely unorganized, so a major role for labour education is to support organizing. Special labour education initiatives are important to reach out to immigrants. Immigrants face language and cultural barriers that must be addressed to effectively organize them. Labour education is also needed to educate existing union leaders and members on the necessity and viability of organizing immigrant workers. Labour education can facilitate developing resources for unions who are organizing immigrant workers. Conferences and workshops are useful for union leaders and organizers to share experiences and learn effective organizing strategies.

In addition labour education is a tool for recruiting and training a new generation of organizers among immigrants themselves, who can bridge the divide between unions and immigrant communities. Labour education must address special concerns of immigrant union members. Some unions have embraced popular education, utilizing linguistically and culturally sensitive ways to address topics including strike preparation, contract bargaining, and building labour and community alliances.

In this chapter, I want to highlight a few of the innovative labour education and organizing initiatives that have strengthened the field of labour education for immigrant workers. It includes the Asian Pacific American Labor Alliance's program for organizing education to recruit and train a new generation of Asian American organizers. It also includes convening educational conferences and developing resources for immigrant worker organizing initiatives in Los Angeles. Finally, it includes the popular education program developed to prepare for the April 2000 strike of the Los Angeles Justice for Janitors Campaign.

Los Angeles has emerged as a focal point of the new US labour movement. In 1999 –2000, more than 100,000 workers joined unions in Los Angeles, an unprecedented increase in recent years. Union membership increased by more than 10 percent,[15] and these victories have established Los Angeles as the national leader in organizing the unorganized. Some of the most innovative organizing campaigns in the country are occurring in Los Angeles, and most of these campaigns involve immigrant workers.

The US labour movement's single largest union victory in decades was won in Los Angeles in 1999, when 74,000 home health care workers joined the Service Employees International Union. The newly organized workers are changing the face of the US labour movement. The ranks of these new union members include more women, more people of colour, and more immigrants than the rest of the workforce and labour movement. These new workers are also predominantly low-wage workers, trapped at the bottom of a labour market where the gap between the rich and poor has grown substantially over the years.

These newly organized workers, particularly immigrant workers, are largely unaware of their rights and of the role of unions. Immigrants frequently have prior experiences with unions from their home countries, sometimes positive and sometimes not. These also need to be addressed in the process of education. In order to strengthen the labour movement, new union members must be educated about their power and the role of collective bargaining and collective action.

In addition to educating recent immigrants, labour education can serve to educate union members and their allies about the potential of immigrant workers. The US labour movement has only recently begun to reach out to immigrants. For generations, the AFL-CIO had been at the forefront in advancing restrictive immigration policies. US unions had traditionally feared immigrant workers would lower their wages and working conditions, and would be used by employers as strikebreakers. In the 1980s, the AFL-CIO advocated for legislation that successfully enacted "employer sanctions," imposing civil and criminal penalties on employers who knowingly hire undocumented immigrant workers.[16]

The intent of employer sanctions was to penalize employers, and therefore, reduce the available jobs that were enticing undocumented workers to enter the country. In reality, it is the workers themselves who have been penalized. The impact of employer sanctions has intensified the exploitation and abuse of immigrant workers. The underground economy has grown, and with it a complete lack of labour standards enforcement. Undocumented workers have virtually no recourse in the face of blatant violations of labour laws, including minimum wage, health and safety, and child labour protections. This exploitation has lowered labour standards for all workers, and made the challenge of

---

[15] *Los Angeles Times,* Jan 20, 2000.

[16] *Los Angeles Times,* June 11, 2000.

unionization more difficult. Thus the traditional anti-immigrant stance of the labour movement has been recently re-evaluated. Labour education directed at union leaders on the organizing potential among immigrant workers, as well as on how the abuse of immigrant workers impacts union workers, played a crucial role in reversing the AFL-CIO's anti-immigrant policies.

In February 2000, the AFL-CIO made a dramatic change with regard to their policy on immigration. By unanimous decision, the AFL-CIO Executive Council passed a resolution calling for a new amnesty program to legalize the estimated six million undocumented immigrants in the country, and to call for the repeal of employer sanctions. This decision sent shock waves through immigrant communities. In a complete role reversal, the AFL-CIO had now positioned itself as one of the major advocates for immigrant rights and immigration law reform in the country.

Between March and June 2000, the AFL-CIO convened a series of four "town hall" meetings around the country to promote awareness among union members and the general public about immigrant workers. The town halls also forged stronger labour and community alliances related to immigrant workers. The largest "town hall" meeting by far was held in Los Angeles, where an overflow crowd of 20,000 workers filled the Los Angeles Sports Arena to rally for immigrant rights, amnesty, and repeal of employer sanctions.

Labour education and the Asian Pacific American Labor Alliance

The Asian Pacific American Labor Alliance (APALA) was formed in 1992 to build a bridge between the labour movement and the Asian American community. From its inception, a major focus of this organization has been to advance the interests of Asian American immigrant workers, who comprise two-thirds of the Asian American work force. Prior to the founding of APALA, the policies of the US labour movement towards Asian American workers had been deplorable. The founding president of the American Federation of Labor, Samuel Gompers, was a lifelong opponent of Asian immigration, and supported restrictive policies that prohibited Asian workers from joining unions (Saxton, 1971, p.271).

Racially restrictive immigration policies were finally eased in the 1960s (Chan, 1991, p.145), and the Asian American population has grown exponentially in the past few decades. Asian Americans are the fastest growing ethnic community in the country, currently exceeding 10 million. In spite of this tremendous growth, the US labour movement has made very little effort to reach out to this new work force.

In 1992, APALA resolved that a major objective would be to recruit a new generation of Asian American union organizers. The dearth of Asian organizers meant that the large and growing Asian immigrant work force was being almost completely ignored by the labour movement. With few exceptions, unions did not have the interest or the capacity to organize Asian American workers. They lacked language and cultural skills to effectively work with Asian immigrant workers and their potential allies.

APALA partnered with the AFL-CIO Organizing Institute (see Widenor and Feekin chapter) to establish a new program specifically to recruit and train new Asian American organizers. The APALA/AFL-CIO Organizing Institute program is a participatory labour education program to recruit, identify, and develop new organizers. The program begins with a three-day training on organizing. The training provides hands-on experience in one-to-one organizing, house-calls, building worker committees, responding to anti-union campaigns, and cultivating community allies. Potential organizers participating in the program are presented with case studies and role-playing where they address the issues of diverse workers, including immigrant workers.

The program also provides an opportunity for union organizers to assess the talents of potential organizers, and exposes participants to the realities of a career in organized labour. Successful graduates of the training are then encouraged to participate in longer-term internships and apprenticeships, where experienced union organizers in the field mentor them. The success of the partnership has also encouraged the AFL-CIO Organizing Institute to initiate similar programs to recruit African American and Latino organizers.

The APALA/AFL-CIO Organizing Institute has yielded impressive results. In 1992 there were fewer than a dozen Asian American union organizers nationally. In the last 10 years, more than 100 Asian American union organizers have been recruited and trained, and the ranks are growing. Many of these organizers are young activists with tremendous enthusiasm and energy, and with a strong commitment to social justice. Through the collective resources of APALA, the US labour movement for the first time has multi-lingual capacity in many Asian languages to assist in translating materials, reaching out to the community, and in organizing immigrant workers.

The APALA national conventions have also been used as an opportunity to promote extensive labour education. The national conventions have been inspirational gatherings, bringing together hundreds of Asian American union activists who often have never before met or interacted with each other. APALA has used these conventions to conduct organizing education, and to encourage rank and file members to become volunteer organizers within their unions. National conventions have trained members on one-on-one organizing, where participants would practice house-calling skills, and sit through mock "captive audience" meetings. At other workshops, organizers have shared organizing strategies, evaluating campaigns that have effectively organized Asian Pacific American workers. In addition, APALA has held strategy sessions to address concerns of organizers themselves, including the challenges facing immigrants, people of colour, women and young people in unions dominated by older white men.

Another exciting development at the APALA national conventions has been the emergence of informal ethnic caucuses, which have provided an opportunity for Chinese, Korean, Filipino, Vietnamese, and other Asian ethnic groups to meet other union activists who speak the same language. The APALA conventions have provided simultaneous interpretation for Asian immigrant workers, something unheard of at most US union conventions. The caucuses have provided education for immigrant workers on how to better access union resources, to demand the right of participation within their unions, and to strengthen labour and community alliances. Through the caucuses, informal mentoring programs have developed, where more seasoned activists have encouraged the development of newer union members. These initiatives have not only strengthened participation by immigrant workers within their unions, but have also encouraged unions to aggressively reach out to unorganized immigrant workers.

APALA has also launched a Campaign for Worker Justice (CWJ) to target key organizing campaigns nationally involving Asian American workers. APALA provides organizing drives with bilingual organizers and translation services to reach diverse populations of Asian immigrant workers. The CWJ also seeks to educate the Asian American community about worker rights and unions, while also training rank and file union activists to participate in broad-based community education.

Labour education and immigrant worker organizing

The University of California at Los Angeles (UCLA) Center for Labor Research has been involved in extensive labour education and research involving immigrant workers in Los Angeles. The last decade has witnessed a series of impressive breakthroughs in organizing immigrant workers. Researching, compiling, and disseminating the stories and strategies of these campaigns are a valuable contribution of labour education to support unions involved in organizing immigrant workers.

The Justice for Janitors campaign of the Service Employees International Union successfully organized thousands of Latino immigrant janitors in Los Angeles in 1990. This union victory brought substantial increases in wages, and for the first time, health benefits for the janitors. Janitorial membership in Los Angeles rose from about 1,800 to 8,000 from the beginning of the campaign to the successful unionization breakthroughs in 1990. This was the largest private-sector union organizing achievement involving Latino immigrants since the United Farm Workers victories nearly two decades earlier (Bronfenbrenner, 1998, p.102).

In July 1990, 1,200 Latino immigrant workers at the American Racing Equipment wheel factory in Los Angeles launched a wildcat strike. The workers had complained about horrible health and safety conditions. In addition, management unilaterally attempted a speed up, forcing workers to work on two machines instead of one. The workers resisted the speed up, and called a strike. The strike was mobilized and led by the workers themselves, independent of any direct union involvement. Subsequently, the International Association of Machinists assisted in the organizing campaign. The workers exhibited tremendous courage and solidarity. In the election held later that year, the workers overwhelming chose union representation. This was the largest factory organized in the Los Angeles area in over 20 years (Milkman, 2000, p.150).

In 1992, thousands of Mexican immigrant construction workers launched a wildcat strike that spread throughout five counties in Southern California. The "drywall workers" who installed sheetrock panels to build homes, had suffered a steady erosion of their wages over the years, and successfully shut down the residential construction industry throughout Southern California. After a five-month strike, the workers prevailed. The resulting contract doubled drywallers' wage rates in Los Angeles and surrounding counties and brought 2,400 workers into the Carpenters' union (Milkman, 2000, p.169).

The UCLA Labor Center documented these stories and compiled them in a book with inspiring photos entitled *Voices from the Front Lines: Organizing Immigrant Workers in Los Angeles* in English and Spanish (Milkman & Wong, 2000). The book features some of the prominent organizers who led these campaigns. This popularly written publication has been a useful document for unions throughout California as an educational tool for their members, and to support future organizing initiatives. The stories of the workers' courage and solidarity inspire other workers who are facing similar struggles to improve their lives. These stories also inspire activists to consider union organizing as a career.

In addition, the Labor Center convened two major conferences on immigrant worker organizing in 1998 and 1999 in Los Angeles. These conferences brought together immigrant worker organizers from various unions for the first time to share their experiences, learn from each others' work, and discuss a common plan of action to strengthen immigrant worker organizing. In a union culture that has kept organizers isolated from each other and competing against each other over jurisdictions, these conferences represented a significant change. The conferences promoted small group discussions, collective problem solving, and relationship building. Although many of these organizers had led incredible campaigns targeting the same Latino immigrant work force, for most this was the first opportunity to meet one another.

The conference also expanded the scope of immigrant worker organizing beyond unions. Invited to participate were other community-based immigrant worker organizing initiatives, including day-labourers who seek work from the street corners of the city, and domestic workers who clean homes. There were also sessions led by immigrant rights advocates who briefed the workers on current efforts to reform federal immigration policy.

These conferences have served to educate both unions and the community about each other's work. Union members learned about community-based organizing campaigns and the work of the immigrant rights advocates. Community advocates learned about the US labour movement's new commitment to organize immigrants. And both union and community organizers learned about winning strategies and shared experiences. A new coalition has emerged between community-based immigrant worker initiatives and unions targeting immigrant workers in the Los Angeles area.

The conferences and coalition-building helped to launch an Immigration Committee within the Los Angeles County Federation of labor, which subsequently spearheaded the above-mentioned town hall on immigrant rights. The committee continues to meet to strategize about how to integrate an immigrant rights agenda within the labour movement, and to support future organizing of immigrants.

Labour education and the Justice for Janitors strike (2000)

In April 2000, one of the most powerful strikes in recent labour history was launched and won by the Service Employees International Union, Local 1877, involving 8,000 janitors in Los Angeles (Institute for Industrial Relations, 2001). The success of this strike was due to the union's early strategic industry research and the subsequent popular education program. For two years, janitors were engaged in a popular education campaign conducted in Spanish including an analysis of who has the power in the building service industry, the economic and political terrain, and the necessity of direct action to win union demands.

The union had done extensive research on the real estate industry in Los Angeles and how the shift to sub-contracting had eroded the wages and working conditions of workers in the industry. In years past, building owners directly hired janitors to clean their buildings and these workers were largely unionized. In the 1970s and 1980s, however, the industry successfully undermined union strength by using non-union building service contractors. The 1990 victory of the janitors regained union strength in the industry, but the union was still lagging behind previous wage and benefit levels enjoyed before the building service industry's transformation.

The union determined that the only way they could make progress at the bargaining table and increase wages beyond the poverty level would be to strike. In addition, they needed to broaden the campaign beyond just targeting the contractors, who serve the role as "middle men," and confront the building owners as well. The union realized that they had to create a "crisis" before the City would respond.

The union embarked on an ambitious bilingual popular education campaign to educate the largely Latino rank and file union membership. Union members were educated about the economic environment, the nature of the commercial real estate industry, and the relations of power among the union, the contractors, and the building owners. They discussed why the union had to strike, and why the union needed to develop strategic allies with community and religious organizations.

This rank and file education program was the key ingredient to the success of the strike. Because the strike involved buildings scattered throughout a huge geographic area in Los Angeles County, the rank and file members had to assume important roles of leadership. Given the nature of the strike, there was no way that the union had sufficient staff and resources to cover every single building location. The extensive rank and file education was the only way to mobilize the workers across the city. Because of the level of worker education and participation, the three-week strike exceeded all expectations, and galvanized rank and file leadership in a way rarely seen in recent decades in the US labour movement.

Striking janitors wore bright red T-shirts with a logo of a clenched fist holding a mop, and bearing the slogan "Justice for Janitors" in bold letters. The T-shirts became a powerful symbol of the strike. Because of the incredible solidarity of these workers, the union was able to keep the strike in the media headlines. Politicians and celebrities were lining up to march with the janitors. Through disseminating research and education, the union was able to win broad public support and project a human face on the strike.

A highlight of the strike occurred when the workers staged a massive 10-mile march from downtown Los Angeles by way of Wilshire Boulevard, passing through the heartland of corporate Los Angeles. Office workers and pedestrians lined the streets to wave and cheer on the janitors, some holding hand made placards in support of the strike, and contributing money on the spot to the strike fund. By the end of the third week, the momentum in support of the union was overwhelming and the janitors won a tremendous victory. The strike also served as a crucial morale boost for the other 250,000 workers in Los Angeles whose contracts expired in 2000, including bus drivers, county workers, teachers, and actors.

Labour education and the road forward

Immigrant workers will continue to play a crucial role in the revitalization of the US labour movement. Labour education must be conducted in a way that builds on the knowledge and experiences of immigrant workers. It must be developed with cultural sensitivity, and provided in languages that immigrants speak. Labour Education must educate existing union leaders and members on the importance of immigrant worker organizing, and the necessity of labour aligning with the immigrant rights community. Popular publications help to capture the voices of the immigrant workers, and promote lessons and experiences. Participatory conferences can also bring diverse groups of unions and community groups together to share experiences, strategize, and develop relationships. Labour education must also include crosscutting programs to foster labour and community coalitions and build strategic alliances.

Labour education should help to ensure that immigrant workers are fully integrated into the labour movement, and to promote democratic participation. This process is essential in developing new leaders and in recruiting and training new organizers. In order to meet the challenges ahead, labour educators must be bold, creative, and aggressive in identifying and meeting the changing needs of the work force. Labour educators must see their roles as teachers, organizers, agitators, and agents of social change.

REFERENCES

* Bronfenbrenner, K. (1998). *Organizing to win: New research on union strategies.* New York: Cornell University.
* Chan, S. (1991). *Asian Americans: An interpretive history.* Los Angeles: Twayne Publishers.
* Institute of Industrial Relations. (2001). *Justice for janitors in Los Angeles: Lessons from three rounds of negotiations.* Los Angeles: UCLA Institute of Industrial Relations Working Paper Series.
* Milkman, R. (2000). *Organizing immigrants: The challenge for unions in contemporary California.* New York: Cornell University.
* Milkman, R. & Wong, K. (2000). *Voices from the front lines: Organizing immigrants in Los Angeles.* Los Angeles: UCLA Labor Center.
* Saxton, A. (1971). *The indispensable enemy: Labor and the anti-Chinese movement in California.* Los Angeles: University of California Press.

7

Research Circles in Sweden: Strengthening the Double Democratic Function of Trade Unions

GUNILLA HÄRNSTEN AND LARS HOLMSTRAND

This chapter looks at the potential for strengthening and democratizing trade unions through research circles. The concept points on the one hand to the idea of making university research accessible to unions and on the other hand to the study circle tradition to which it is closely related. Research circles have been used by and for Swedish trade unions for almost 25 years and clearly belong to the labour education tradition. They may be one possible answer to the current challenges trade unions are facing. Since research circles can be used to address a wide variety of issues at different levels of union activity, they are worth looking at from both a democratic and liberatory perspective.

Background

In Sweden, the trade unions are usually considered to be exceptionally strong and important. In at least one sense, this is accurate – the membership ratio is very high, with current figures at 82 percent (85 percent among blue-collar workers and 80 among white-collar workers; see www.dn.se/jobb, 2000-09-24).

Kjellberg (2000) describes the politically and religiously homogeneous unions in the Nordic countries (Denmark, Finland, Norway and Sweden) as clearly different from the unions of other continental European countries even if there is a substantial degree of variation among them. Nordic unions enjoy strikingly high membership, strong collective bargaining power and an influential position within the domain of labour law. In Sweden, the Co-Determination Act and the Work Environment Act resulted from the proactive role Swedish unions played during the 1970s.

The two large trade union confederations are The Swedish Confederation of Trade Unions (LO) and The Swedish Confederation of Professional Employees (TCO). The former consists of 20 blue-collar unions with a combined 2.3 million members. The LO is the original trade union organization with a historical record of struggle, not least at the workplace level. However, over time it has become more bureaucratic and linked to the state and the Social Democratic Party. The TCO consists of 20 white-collar unions with 1.2

million members. This confederation was formed in the 1940s and has among its members clerical workers, secretaries, teachers, and engineers. It might be described as heterogeneous and somewhat lacking in collective traditions. The TCO is independent from political party affiliation. The LO and the TCO have the same basic internal organizational structure, based on the tradition of representative democracy and having a hierarchical construction with at least three levels (local, regional and national).

In the 21st century, Sweden is rapidly moving towards a more segregated and market-oriented system. In consequence, the general position of Swedish trade unions in relation to both employers and politics has been weakened. A partly connected problem has occurred in union internal democracy: the lack of engagement and involvement by the members in the union organization. At the root of this is the overemphasis of the representative, rather than the participatory, aspects of union democracy. Young people seem to be demanding a more membership-oriented union, as are women and members in small workplaces. They want a bottom-up, goal-oriented social movement rather than a hierarchical organization. Kjellberg (1997) recommends a strategy of moving towards a more decentralized, member oriented and informal union to meet the challenges of a new economy.

The research circle

First developed as an arena for co-operation between universities and trade unions during the second half of the 1970s, the research circle can be regarded as a democratic invention aimed at making results from university research more accessible to trade unions. Although research circles have operated for more than two decades across Sweden, there has been a contemporary revitalization of the study circle tradition (Holmstrand, 1993; Holmstrand & Härnsten, 1992; Holmstrand et al., 1994; Härnsten, 1994).

A research circle is formed by adding one or more researchers to a study circle in which an issue or problem, identified by the participants, is under scrutiny. In most cases the research circles have been initiated by or channelled through the unions, and they have dealt with a great variety of working life issues of importance for the unions and their members. These circles have provided an opportunity for different kinds of knowledge to converge. Thus the scientific and theoretical knowledge of researchers integrates with the experiential and practical knowledge of ordinary working people. At its best, the research circles have inspired a constructive dialogue and a knowledge growth where both parties have learned a great deal from each other.

A democratic view on knowledge rests among other things on the humanistic conception of the equal value of all human beings and also on the firm belief, supported by scientific findings, that there is a great unexploited human potential for learning (Häyrynen & Hautamäki, 1976; Bloom, 1985). Another assumption is that all human beings are curious and actively and creatively seek knowledge. An important aspect of this democratic perspective of knowledge is the recognition of several different types of knowledge, e.g. vocational, everyday, scientific and artistic (Tengström, 1986). Another widely discussed concept in working life research is tacit knowledge.

The dominant view in the scientific context as well as in society at large seems to imply that the knowledge of experts – researchers and other formally competent persons – weighs heavier than the experiential knowledge of those without this level of formal education. In this dominant view there is an exaggerated belief in the precedence of scientific knowledge and as a consequence, an elitist conception of knowledge. The democratic view of knowledge challenges this perspective and points to the necessity of including other perspectives and the experiences of as many people as possible.

According to Freire (1970, 1972), the structures that prevent people from participating in decisions concerning their own lives create a culture of silence. To combat this silence, he calls for a demystification of popular understandings, which must be combined with scientific criticism of reality developed in co-operation between scientists and practitioners. But this scientific knowledge should not be uncritically transmitted. A problem emphasized by Freire is that many scientists have a very limited and also erroneous picture of reality, a consequence of social structures including rigid divisions of labour. Given these constraints, it is difficult for an authentic dialogue to develop between people with different knowledge and experiences. Consequently there is a need for creating new arenas. The research circle is one answer to this kind of need. Below we will review some examples of creating and using such arenas to stimulate what we call democratic knowledge processes. The intention is to provide the participants in the research circles with opportunities to deepen their knowledge and thus strengthen the unions.

Three research circles

Our examples of research circles from different contexts all take the democratic perspective of knowledge and focus on important issues in Swedish working life. The first example is of a research circle of parents who want to influence their children's schooling. The second example concerns the work environment of cleaners. The third example is a research circle revolving around the Swedish welfare sector and the European Community: in the latter research circle, the main issue was whether or not the EC was a threat to this sector.

1. Research circles preparing parents for participation in the school

An initiative from a labour movement representative in the Middle Sweden region provided an opportunity to start research circles around developing the school system in a more democratic and egalitarian direction. One of us was invited to participate in a research circle with the theme "Education – of course, but for whom and about what?" Several people with local labour movement connection gathered. They included members of the local board of education, teachers of folk high school (a Scandinavian adult education institution, initiated in Denmark), educators in popular movements such as environmental groups, and trade union educators. This circle had seven meetings over a half-year.

An important purpose of the circle was to bring together different radical educational traditions in the region. The heterogeneity of the circle was a problem but was overcome through the circle discussions. The circle concluded its work with a recommendation to try to start research circles with parents of children who would begin school in the coming year. This plan was launched in connection with local development work initiated by the LO and as a result, several parents formed a new research circle to continue the work.

This research circle observed that all their jobs demanded a substantial knowledge base, and that this knowledge base was continually increasing. It was also clear to them that most skills and knowledge needed in their daily jobs had been acquired after the school years – and sometimes in spite of the impact of the school!

One of the first sessions was devoted to discussions based on memories from everyone's school years. From these discussions, it became obvious that school had been a negative experience for many participants in the circle. Images of oppression in different forms, and the aggressiveness of the school environment as a whole stood out clearly. For many, school was something to endure in order to finally leave and get a job.

Discussions within the circle produced insights and action. It became clear that in order to enhance democratic development within the school, co-operation by interested parents would be beneficial. Another important discussion in the circle concerned the links between the school and working life. Participants in the circle realized that the knowledge of all working parents is a great non-explored resource that could be used by school personnel and the children in a positive developmental spiral. The mutual benefit of change for the school and the working life in a community became indisputable. As a result of the research circle, a person was employed at the upper level of the comprehensive school with the task of developing co-operation between the school and the community.

The important achievement of this circle was that it managed to put the issues under discussion in the light of a wider social context. The theories of Bernstein (1977) and Negt (1974; 1987) were very useful for this group of parents. The meetings of the circle did not result in any fast and easy solutions, but did reveal which strategies were necessary. The parents in the circle demonstrated that their insights could change things. The research attracted interest from both the central and local levels within LO and within educational bodies (Härnsten, 1995).

2. The research circle of cleaners

This research circle consisted of a group of 10 cleaners, all women working at the same hospital in a small town in the middle of Sweden. The initiative to form the circle was taken by the local union, which for a long time had tried to get the employer to examine and improve working conditions. Working conditions were characterized by hierarchical organization, little influence, very low status for the employees and a high rate of work injuries. All women were members of the Swedish Communal Workers' Union, but with little participation and interest in union work.

When the circle began, some time was devoted to mapping out and clearly describing the work done by each woman. In so doing, the women became "experts" in the area they cleaned and in the way they were doing it. To talk about the daily work and to listen to their co-workers was an important element in the circle work. The self-confidence of the cleaners was also enhanced by the fact that a researcher was listening and taking very seriously everything they said.

The participants of this circle were interested in good examples of better working conditions. They were convinced that their situation was worse than normal. A study visit to a workplace with a good reputation in a neighbouring town clearly proved, however, that the measures taken there were mostly cosmetic. Participants also read about several attempts at making workplace improvements, but that did not provide any directly applicable or useful ideas. However, by finding out about the experiences of other people in similar work situations, it became quite clear to participants that the problems are more or less the same for most employees, even if on the surface they may seem to be somewhat different. This insight encouraged the circle to go further. With recommendations from a professor of industrial ergonomics as a starting point and based on calculations made from their own knowledge and experience concerning the area to be cleaned, the group prepared a proposal for a new work organization. The proposal was based on the premise that the cleaners would gradually pursue their own course of action and that they would also be responsible for their own budget. Calculations showed that job absenteeism due to work injuries cost so much that two more full-time jobs could be added if the work injuries were eventually eliminated. In the new work schedule, the cleaners themselves decided how to distribute the time needed to clean the various areas. In the total working time, a daily half-hour of group planning was included, as well as physical exercises twice a week and vocational and social education for all members of the group (19 days per year as recommended by LO).

The above proposal for a new work organization was introduced at a meeting with the hospital director, a work supervisor, the company nurse and a politician (a social democrat). All of them initially stated that they approved of the proposal the research circle had made. However, when it was suggested that time for physical exercise and education was required, the figures that showed how costly the injured staff was, were not considered directly relevant. Even the plan outlined for education of the whole group was questioned. The cleaners left the meeting with several questions unanswered.

The cleaners continued to organize and press their demands. A short while after the circle work finished, the cleaners received increased wages and their story was featured on local TV and in the union journal. They got the demanded education through a nearby folk high school.

Three years after the research circle ended, the cleaning centre looked different. The women had their own budget, they planned the areas to be cleaned, they were given new equipment and they had time for studies and physical exercise. Work injuries decreased to a considerable extent. On the other hand, they still considered themselves a very vulnerable group when it came to restructuring and replacements. Their feeling of being at the bottom of the hierarchy and exposed to the discretion of "the big shots" remained. (For a fuller account, see Härnsten, 1994; Holmstrand & Härnsten, 1996).

After several organizational changes, the cleaning centre was closed. The cleaners were relocated to other workplaces, received early retirement or were laid off. The change in workplace conditions that they managed to achieve could not resist the political and economic changes that occurred in Sweden during the 1990s.

3. Research circles about the Swedish welfare sector

Two research circles in Uppsala were in operation during the second half of the 1980s around issues threatening the Swedish welfare sector, or "common sector" as it is also called. The initiatives and the union participants came from the local LO unions of the Uppsala region, with members employed by the local administrations (the "Communes") or the different state authorities in the area.

The first circle dealt with the problem of privatization of different kinds, which began to be a hotly debated theme during the early 1980s. It was claimed by the critics of the welfare sector that this sector was ineffective, bureaucratic and too costly. One proposed way of getting more and better use of tax-payers' money was to privatize parts of the work organized and run by the local administrations, such as collecting garbage, cleaning the offices or day-care for pre-school children.

The research circle used the rich experiences of the participants, the contributions of guest researchers and local administrators, research literature and union material to critically and self-critically scrutinize the issues. The conclusion reached by the circle, however, was very clear-cut. When comparing the alternatives of conducting a certain kind of work within the common sector with a private alternative with all economic conditions comparable and calculated the same way, the private alternative always was estimated to be more expensive because of the need to a make profit.

The second circle grew out of the first, and started with the provocative question of whether the European Community (EC) should be looked upon as "a gigantic privatization threat." The circle started by inviting a lecturer in Political Science to provide an overview of the European Community with its history, institutions, procedures for decision-making and so on. They also read what accessible literature there was concerning the EC and took part in different seminars and conferences. Political journalists and unionists of various kinds were questioned by the participants about their views on the EC either at circle meetings or on other occasions. The participants even contacted union colleagues in other countries within the EC to find out about their experiences.

One of the most fruitful ingredients of the circle work was a study visit to Brussels in April 1990, where there was an opportunity to interview key persons and get direct impressions of the EC. After this visit, the circle concentrated its work on analyzing and discussing the rich material that had been gathered. The participating researcher prepared a report, and the circle participants discussed versions of it.

The report expressed scepticism towards the EC and a critical attitude to the prospect of Swedish membership in it. In fact, circle participants found many reasons to doubt whether the welfare models in the EC countries and the welfare politics of the EC itself really were compatible with the Swedish welfare model. To this they also added the foreseeable costs for Sweden in joining the Community and, not least, the apparent lack of democracy in the EC. The research circle therefore arrived at their answer to the initial question about the whether the EC was "a gigantic welfare threat" with a "yes." The report was widely circulated within the Communal Workers' Union. However, the Swedish referendum resulted in a small but clear "yes" to joining the EC, and all the misgivings the circle had turned out to be justified.

Discussion

A central ingredient in what Freire calls a pedagogy of the oppressed consists in training people to continuously reassess, to analyze discoveries, to use scientific methods and processes and to perceive themselves in a dialectical relationship to their social reality. By developing such an education, people could be helped to take a more critical stance towards the world and thereby change it.

In all three circles the reality of the participants and their own knowledge and experience were used to a large extent. Various theoretical perspectives were presented by the researchers and widely discussed by the participants at the circle meetings. Most importantly these different kinds of knowledge were integrated and developed into new and deeper insights in each research circle. Broader perspectives were integrated into the thoughts of the participants and there was often a growing consciousness of the complexities of larger contexts.

The German sociologist Oskar Negt has used his experiences with industrial workers as the basis for developing a pedagogical approach in the same vein as Freire (see for example Negt, 1974; 1987). Interestingly, Negt emphasizes the important role of the trade unions as a social movement. He regards them as an inherently democratizing force, provided they can develop their internal democracy and thereby strengthen their external power. The research circles have the potential to directly influence this double democratic function of trade unions. It is reasonable, at least in principle, to classify research circles as either "emancipatory" or "strategic." The line of demarcation can naturally be fluent. The first type of circle is the one that primarily addresses participants "at the bottom of the hierarchy," groups that are relatively poorly educated and with a low status. The other type of research circle addresses participants a bit higher up in the union organization and deals with issues of strategic importance for the trade union movement. The emancipatory research circle contributes above all to the development and vitalization of the internal democracy of the unions, while the strategic circle primarily strengthens the external democracy – it increases the ability of the unions to put forward well-founded demands for reforms in working life and society.

When we look at our research circle examples we find that the first one must be considered as above all emancipatory: the participants who were able to deal with their school experiences formulated and expressed their own views. Step by step, they developed a wider perspective with this basis. But this can also be seen as an example of strategic research circles in the union perspective. Thus the results from these circles are increasingly used strategically, with the report distributed and discussed within the LO unions. The second example of research circles is similar. But the third example must be labelled a strategic research circle. The issue under scrutiny was evidently one of the most complex and general so far treated in a research circle. And the results of the circle's work were considered to be of great strategic importance and worthy of disseminating within the LO unions.

With the above examples, we want to emphasize the inherent strength of research circles as a tool for unions to develop their democratic potential. The robustness and simplicity of the basic idea allows research circles to be adapted to and used for a great variety of issues, ranging from a narrow work environment problem to a more complex and strategic problems of national welfare systems. All circles contained empowering and emancipatory elements that did contribute to enhanced internal democracy of the unions. In many research circles there is also a more or less apparent strategic perspective in the sense that the results of the circle work could be used to form union policy. In some cases the strategic aspect can be present from the beginning and may concern more comprehensive issues. In these cases, we can talk about research circles that have a role in the external democratic function of the union. These examples of research circles are chosen to illustrate how the union members operated. They do not romanticize the impact that research circles can have; social change requires political and social action on a broader scale.

In the Swedish trade union movement, there is a strong tendency to over-emphasize the formal aspects of the representative system. In practice this means that too much responsibility is taken away from the grass-root levels and given to the upper hierarchies of the union. The view of knowledge we have described and systematically applied in our circle work represents a democratic perspective that challenges some aspects of this union tradition.

REFERENCES

• Bernstein , B. (1977). *Class, codes and control. Volume 3. Towards a theory of educational transmissions.* London: Routledge and Kegan Paul.

• Bloom, B.S. (1985). *Developing talent in young people.* New York: Ballantine Books.

• Forrester, K. & Thorne, C. (Eds). (1993). *Trade unions and social research.* Aldershot: Avebury.

• Freire, P. (1972). *Cultural action for freedom.* Cambridge, Mass.: Center for the Study of Development and Change.

• Freire, P. (1970). *Pedagogy of the oppressed.* New York: Herder and Herder.

• Gam, P., Gullichsen, A., Toumisto, J. & Klason, M. (1992). *Social change and adult education research – Adult education research in Nordic countries 1990/91.* Linköping: Linköping University.

• Härnsten, G. (1995). Den långa vägen till föräldrainflytande. (The long way to parent influence.) Rapport från två forskningscirklar kring arbetarrörelsen och skolan. ALFOFAK-rapport nr 3. *Pedagogisk forskning i Uppsala 125.* Uppsala: pedagogiska institutionen.

• Härnsten, G. (1994). *The research circle – Building knowledge on equal terms.* Stockholm: LO.

• Häyrynen, Y.P. & Hautamäki, J. (1976). *Människans bildbarhet och utbildningspolitiken.* (The educability of man and the educational politics.) Stockholm: Wahlström & Widstrand.

• Holmstrand, L. & Härnsten, G. (1996). Democratic knowledge processes in working life. Paper presented at the Fourth Conference on Learning and Research in Working Life, Steyr, Austria, July 1-4 1996.

• Holmstrand, L. (1990). *EG – ett hot mot den offentliga sektorn.* (The EC – a threat against the welfare sector.) Uppsala: LO-distriktet & Uppsala universitet.

• Holmstrand, L., Lindström, K., Löwstedt, J. & Englund, A. (1994). The research circle – a model for collaborative learning at work. Paper presented at the international conference on Learning at work, Lund, June 1994.

• Holmstrand, L. (1993). The research circle – A way of co-operating. In Forrester & Thorne, *Trade unions and social research.* Aldershot Avebury. ss 106-114.

• Holmstrand, L. & Härnsten, G. (1992). The research circle – Some educational perspectives. In Gam et al., *Social change and adult education research – Adult education research in Nordic countries*. Linköping: Linköping University. 1992, ss 230-242.

• Kjellberg, A. (1997). *Fackliga organisationer och medlemmar i dagens Sverige.* (Trade unions and members in today's Sweden.) Lund: Arkiv Förlag.

• Kjellberg, A. (2000). *Facklig organisering och partsrelationer i Sverige och Danmark.* (Trade union organization and industrial relations in Sweden and Denmark.) In: Ibsen, I. & Scheuer, S. (red.) *Septemberforliget og det 21. Århundrede.* Köpenhamn: Jurist- og Ökonomiforbundets Forlag, ss 53-68.

• Negt, O. (1987). *Levande arbete, stulen tid.* (Living work, stolen time.) Göteborg: Röda bokförlaget.

• Negt, O. (1974). *Sociologisk fantasi og exemplarisk indlaering.* (Sociological imagination and exemplary learning.) Roskilde: RUC förlag.

• Tengström, E. (1986). *Myten om informationssamhället – ett humanistiskt inlägg i framtidsdebatten.* (The myth of the information society – a humanistic contribution to the debate about the future.) Stockholm: Rabén & Sjögren.

8

Basic Skills and Union Activity in the UK and Australia

CHRIS HOLLAND AND GERALDINE CASTLETON

The adult language and literacy education field in the UK and Australia has historically had to fight hard for funding and other support to develop programs in the community and in the workplace. In the last decade, policy changes bringing support to basic skills in both countries have been welcomed, first in Australia and later in the UK. The long struggle for recognition, followed by a policy emphasis on the economic more than the social benefits of adult language and literacy (known as "basic skills" in the UK), has impacted on the capacity of adult educators to engage in debates about concepts, principles, policy and best practice. Similarly, trade unions have had to fight hard for their survival. They have recently won inclusion in government funded strategies to develop workplace basic skills. While neither literacy practitioners nor union representatives would argue against increased funding and other support for basic skills, some might argue against the direction this education has taken, and the heavy influence of an economically focused industrial reform agenda.

In Australia, there has been an awareness of the need for language and literacy support in the community and the workplace since 1991. The country undertook a national survey of adult literacy in 1989, and the results were published in 1990, International Literacy Year in the Wickert Report (see Wickert & Zimmerman, 1991, for summary). It was on the basis of these results, indicating that around 10 percent of the adult population had low literacy levels, that adult literacy provision was funded through Australia's Language and Literacy Policy the following year. The funding included initiatives such as the Workplace Language and Literacy (WELL) program.

This new policy, in particular the part that addressed adult language and literacy concerns, formed part of what became known as the National Training Reform Agenda that has shaped a period of change and development in vocational training and education and industrial relations. This period of reform, begun in Australia in the late 1980s, continues to the present day.

The Australian report *Words at Work* (1991) presented a foreboding picture of Australian industry, placing responsibility for its demise on its workers:

> There is now general agreement that Australia needs a more flexible and highly skilled workforce capable of maximizing its productivity, producing quality goods and innovatively exploiting both new technologies and market opportunities. In the drive to

achieve these results it has been apparent that poor literacy, numeracy and English language skills of a significant number of adults and youth is an impediment to this occurring. (p.5)

The UK government's interest in basic skills, although more limited in investment, goes back to 1975-76, when the UK government of the time set up a resource agency, the Adult Literacy and Basic Skills Unit (ALBSU), now known as the Basic Skills Agency (BSA). The BSA definition of basic skills, widely accepted within government and post-16 education in the UK, is similar to the way in which literacy has been defined in Australian policy documents: "the ability to read, write and speak in English, and to use mathematics at a level necessary to function at work and in society in general" (Moser, 1999, p.2). Hamilton (1996) comments that a functional view of literacy focusing on social control and what adults *cannot* do has predominated in the United Kingdom, and this is true also of the Australian context (Castleton, 2000). Hamilton further observes that because arrangements for "English for speakers of other languages" provision have been developed by the Home Office as a response to immigration, approaches to language and literacy tend to be functional, instrumental, and undifferentiated (Hamilton, 1996, p.251).

In 1998, the results of the International Adult Literacy Survey were disseminated. Australia and the UK had participated in the survey, and the results in both countries were initially greeted with outrage and shock. The UK government, partly in response to the findings, commissioned Sir Claus Moser, chairperson of the Basic Skills Agency, to co-ordinate a report on adult basic skills. It was published in 1999. Entitled *A Fresh Start: Improving Literacy and Numeracy,* it has formed the basis of much policy development in adult basic skills and workplace basic skills.

This chapter outlines Australian and UK basic education policy responses to global market competition. It comments on trade union practice in the light of a corporate business agenda that is dominating the application of literacy initiatives in the workplace.

The scale of the problem

The Moser report begins by looking at the "scale of the problem," and offers examples of massive reading deficits in the population, which it attributes to home circumstances and poor schooling, inconsistent national standards, poor motivation and poor promotion of education and training (now generically referred to as "learning") programs.

This report, and previous commissioned reports of the 1990s (eg. Kennedy, 1997; Fryer, 1997), use the language of social justice such as "widening participation" and "combating exclusion." In the Moser report, this language supports a bid to achieve a greater competitive advantage for the UK through training and education. Achieving better basic skills for UK citizens and workers, the report asserts, "must be a national and ongoing crusade" (Moser, 1999, p.4). Empowerment is social inclusion, and social inclusion is employability (Blunkett in DfEE, 1999):

> It is only right that those who missed out early in life should have free access to acquiring the basic tools necessary for their lives. Every citizen with worries about literacy or numeracy should have a clear entitlement to a choice of opportunities for learning and indeed access to a wide variety of study programmes (p.11).

And

> It is generally agreed that, if we are to achieve a world-class economy, we need a world-class workforce. To achieve this, employees and job applicants need good basic skills, not just for the current job, but also for changing demands of employment (p.25).

In Australia and the UK, policy documents seem to have integrated social and economic objectives. There has been some debate in academic and professional journals and conferences about issues such as the effect of workplace change on literacy practices, and about cultural diversity, critical literacy, active citizenship and participatory education. However, these dialogues have not necessarily resulted in any noticeable change in policy and government approaches to these issues. Analysis of workplace literacy programs in Australia (Castleton, 2000) shows that these programs are still largely driven by a functional, skill-based literacy discourse.

Government responses to the problem

Australia has been involved in considerable activity in the area of workplace-based basic skills since the early 1990s. This activity was given a boost through the establishment of the Australian National Training Authority (ANTA), the body responsible for vocational education and training in Australia. Its first and its most recent strategic plan identified the importance of basic skills in developing a more skilled and flexible Australian workforce. Furthermore, ANTA has called for the effective integration of English language, literacy and numeracy training into vocational education and training products (ANTA, 1998, p.14).

Vocational education and training in Australia is now largely centred on Training Packages, a set of national training resources that registered training organizations can use as the basis for their training programs in specific industry areas. These packages contain endorsed and consistent competency standards, assessment guidelines and qualification levels that align with the Australian Qualification Framework (AQF). In official terms, literacy is integrated into these competency standards, though in practice this requisite is not consistent across packages, varying from very explicit statements in some competency standards to more implicit understandings of literacy in others. Many adult literacy practitioners are concerned about the effects of this varying visibility of literacy and the consequence of limited support offered to trainees and employees with literacy needs.

Furthermore, there is growing concern over a noticeable decrease in activity in the adult literacy field in Australia. While some programs, including WELL, continue to be funded, much of the literacy provision and research established in 1991 in the wake of the Australian Language and Literacy Programme (ALLP) is slowly disappearing. The conservative coalition government has established a literacy and numeracy-training program for the young and long-term unemployed, but this program has specific employment-related outcomes and is tied in with mutual obligation responsibilities, so it is hardly seen as providing a worthwhile incentive for people to seek literacy support.

In the UK, the Department of Education and Employment (DfEE) recently established the Adult Basic Skills Strategy. A 150 million-pound investment in basic skills was announced in October 2000, bringing the total investment to more than 247 million pounds since 1999. Measures have included the development of a new national adult basic skills curriculum, consistent qualifications for basic skills, a training framework for trainee and existing teachers, and funding to support the expansion of basic skills learning in the community and workplace.

Information technology is seen as a key to increasing learning opportunities. The University for Industry was established in 1998 to provide access and guidance to learners and to drive up demand for basic skills and IT. Also the professionalization of teachers is receiving more attention, with new, separate standards for basic skills teachers being established. The BSA is reviewing its current basic skills teaching qualifications and has developed intensive training for all basic skills tutors so that they can effectively deliver the new adult basic skills literature.

A three million pound initiative was established for workplace basic skills by the DfEE in 1999 to "build capacity" in face-to-face workplace basic skills on-site provision throughout the country. The Workplace Basic Skills Network (WBSN), based at Lancaster University, is funded by the DfEE mainly to promote good practice and awareness of workplace basic skills, mainly through professional development programs. The Network recently managed a tendering process for one million pounds of government funds to support new and existing basic skills project development around the country.

As well as proposing a range of new organizations and initiatives to address basic skills "deficits," the Moser report has recommended that the TUC and individual unions should be co-opted to negotiate training with employers and colleges. The government has set up a Union Learning Fund for this purpose.

The trade union response

Historically, there have been several shifts in the direction of labour education programs to secure the survival of the movement. In the UK in the 1830s, the Owenites and Chartists were concerned with radical education of the working-class towards social reform and political action, but by the 1840s Chartism had been defeated, and working-class education:

> increasingly turned away from political to economic solutions – how to obtain a share of the profits of capitalism rather than how to overthrow it...The notion of an alternative working-class education was replaced by demands for more equal access to facilities provided by and for the middle class and by the State (Fieldhouse, 1996, p. 17).

In the post-war period the TUC came to see training as a way of weeding out more radical elements and improving representatives' ability to negotiate with management and government.

Trade union development and involvement in labour education programs, described by Gough Whitlam (1997), an ex-labour Prime Minister, as "the labour movement's oldest and best traditions," has declined more recently in Australia. The Trade Union Training Authority undertook work-floor training for union officials and members, but never seriously addressed the issue of basic education skills.

The introduction of programs such as WELL increased the role trade union councils and individual unions played in the establishment of language and literacy programs in workplaces. The union movement had advocated for these programs, seeing an important need arising out of changes to Australia's Industrial Relations Act (1988) that saw the introduction of enterprise (local) bargaining. Unionists recognized that within this process many workers, particularly those of non-English speaking backgrounds and native speakers with limited literacy skills, might be disadvantaged. Union involvement in workplace basic skills was to improve members' abilities to understand the implications of enterprise bargaining.

It was a requirement of early workplace-based literacy programs such as WELL that they be managed by a consultative committee that included union representation. Furthermore, state-based advisory committees that managed these programs on behalf of the federal government included union representation in their membership. The success of the early implementation of the WELL program was largely attributed to the tripartite arrangements in place at enterprise level between unions, employers and providers (Bayliss, 1995).

Today some state-based committees no longer contain union representation, and with the rise in the number of non-union worksites, there is now limited union representation on workplace-based consultative committees. This predicament is, among other things, a reflection of the demise and preoccupations of unions in Australia during this period (discussed in Newman's chapter). These preoccupations meant that unions perhaps missed critical opportunities to have significant input into *how* workplace-based basic skills should be formulated and delivered. A consequence of this has been a lack of appropriate, sustained representation and protection for those who are most vulnerable in today's workplaces – low-skilled workers.

Of concern to literacy practitioners has to be reports that many workers who attended early workplace language and literacy programs have long since been sacked by the very companies initially applauded for the way in which they supported the literacy concerns of their workers. This point emphasizes concerns made by a trade union official some years ago that neither workplace literacy practitioners, nor workers for that matter, truly appreciated the political and industrial complexities of basic skills workplace-based education (Castleton, 1997). In writing about this issue Lankshear (1994) has warned that workplace educators are stepping into:

> Profoundly ideological terrain [which involves participation in] historical and cultural processes that shape how people will live their lives and that they become (and not become); which influence the opportunities that are and are not available to particular people; and which encourage learners to perceive and understand the world and their locations and situations within it in particular ways (p. 107).

In conjunction with the effects of globalization and increased technology in the workplace, the basic skills support function of unions in Australia and the UK is a catalyst for furthering the economic reform process in many enterprises, promoting the development of a training culture. It is the impact of the Total Quality Management discourse and accompanying changing work practices and accountability requirements that have provided the greater impetus for workplace literacy programs, rather than equipping members to cope with the demands of industrial relations issues and enterprise bargaining.

It is clear that the recent Moser Report in the UK has a distinctive, well-defined role for unions in mind in the development of basic skills among adults than was ever conceived for Australian unions in policy documents. This role has been made palatable through the weakened bargaining position of unions in the UK. The Moser report recommended that unions provide basic-skills programs for their members based on the new National Strategy, that they should work with the TUC to train and develop "union learning representatives" who would support and advise learners, and work with employers on the development of basic skills provision in the workplace.

The TUC argues that the unique position of confidence and trust that the union and its representatives have in the workplace means that they have the powerful potential to reach learners with basic skills needs who do not open up to employers or others (such as providers). The TUC works with employer associations, associated trade unions and local colleges to develop suitable basic skills programs. The TUC sees this work as giving workers a voice: "the learners involved with the project are a group that effectively have no voice –

these partnerships are redressing this imbalance and giving them a chance to acquire this voice and vital skills" (Swift, 2000).

Summary and conclusions

While Australia and the UK are at different stages of workplace basic skills development and of union and government support for this work, there seem to be some common, positive outcomes of union involvement. The profile of basic skills has been raised for the population at large and with employers specifically, who are more aware of how they can access provision for their workers. Provider organizations such as technical and further education colleges find it much easier to access money for basic skills in the community and workplace. Partnerships between funders, local and national agencies, providers, business and unions have helped spread information, support, expertise and resources. Workers have found it easier to access basic skills education at work.

To reserve applause for all this work seems churlish. Indeed, if there *are* any doubts about the extent of "illiteracy" and the damage it does to the economy, about the type of provision recommended and funded, about the claims made in regard to what basic skills can achieve for the nation and individuals and about who is responsible for the "problem" of basic skills, such doubts have been given little voice in Australia or within the current campaign in the UK.

Developments in Australia should be a signal to unions in the UK. The early intention of union activity in the WELL program to protect members' interests has not been realized. For instance, workplace language and literacy programs aimed at informing workers about enterprise bargaining have become tools of a competitiveness agenda. Job security of workers has not been increased. In the UK, where a focus on workplace basic skills has come relatively late, the goal of making industry and the country more competitive has been explicit from the outset. Employability, rather than secure employment, has been the vision.

The pace of change has been so fast, the arguments so persuasive, and access to alternative perspectives so limited, that those in the field and the wider public seldom have the opportunity to critique policy and practice before it is enacted (Castleton, 2000; Holland, 2000). From policy implementation to development of practice in institutions and workplaces, the nature of basic skills education remains largely unchallenged. Castleton's (2000) research into workplace literacy in Australia demonstrates how effective such a "buy in" to a deficit model can become in helping to formulate new but limited understandings about the role of literacy at work that then inform further policy and practice.

The opportunity for the TUC, and unions generally, to negotiate the way in which they could take an effective part in the government basic skills revolution is limited. One way in which unions could contribute to a more empowering literacy provision is to work to integrate basic skills with other union learning as well as vocational training, and with learning for active citizenship.

In order to better advocate for the rights and needs of those targeted for basic skills, a more critical, independent involvement in developing workers' basic skills informed by comparative research and development in and beyond the UK and Australia is needed. We need to explore, document and share knowledge about the long-term social and economic benefits accrued through language and literacy education in these countries and elsewhere. We need to be aware of and discuss other interpretations of "the problem" and alternative approaches to literacy development, rather than accept an economically motivated, quantity driven approach.

For unions in particular this means a new era of organized labour, described by Kinchloe in his discussion of the foundations of work and vocational education (1999, p. 325) as "a more critical form of unionism that comprehends the power of corporations." He describes this as meaning that unions must develop a theory of the world that allows workers to arrange and interpret their working lives, rather than have these driven by the business ideology. As teachers, managers, union officials and representatives we need to re-assume a stronger advocacy role by informing ourselves, developing our own research and implementing programs which explore the extent to which workplace basic skills can bring about social as well as economic reform and active rather than functional citizenship.

REFERENCES

- ANTA (1998). *A bridge to the future: The Australian National Training Authority's national strategy for vocational education and training 1998 – 2003.* Brisbane: Australian National Training Authority.

- Bayliss, P. (1995). *Post implementation review of the WELL program under the ALLP.* Canberra: Department of Employment Education & Training.

- BSA Newletters (1992-1999).

- Castleton, G. (1997). *Accounting for policy and practice in workplace literacy: (E)merging discourses on work.* Unpublished PhD thesis. Brisbane: Griffith University.

- Castleton, G. (2000). Workplace literacy: Examining the vitual and vituous realities in (e)merging discourses on work. *Discourse: Studies in the Cultural Politics of Education,* 1 8(2), 91-104.

- DfEE (1998). *The learning age: A renaissance for a new Britain.* London: The Stationary Office

- Fieldhouse, R. (Ed.) (1996). *A modern history of adult education.* NIACE: Leicester.

- Fryer, R. (1997). *Learning for the twenty-first century: First report of the National Advisory Group for Continuing Education and Lifelong Learning* (NAGCELL). London: Government Stationary Office.

- Hamilton, M. (1996). Adult literacy and basic education. In R. Fieldhouse (ed.), *A modern history of adult education*. NIACE: Leicester.

- Holland, C. (2000). *Reflections on empowerment, workplace language and literacy policy, and professional development in England*. Working Knowledge Conference: UTS, Sydney.

- Kennedy, H. (1997). *Learning works: Widening participation in further education*. Coventry: FEFC.

- Kinchloe, J. (1999). *How do we tell the workers? The socioeconomic foundations of work and vocational education*. Boulder, Col: Westview Press.

- Lankshear, C. (1994). Self-directions and empowerment: Critical language awareness and the "new work order." In P. O'Connor (Ed.) *Thinking work volume 1: Theoretical perspectives on workers' literacies*. Sydney: Adult Literacy and Basic Skills Action Coalition.

- Moser, C. (1999). *A fresh start: Improving literacy and numeracy*. Sheffield: DfEE.

- Swift, J. (2000). *Workplace basic skills funding*. Conference presentation, May 2000, TUC.

- Whitlam, G. (1997). Launch of the trade union education foundation. 9 February,

- Wickert, R. & Zimmerman, J. (1991). Adult basic education in Australia: Questions of integrity. In Tennant, M. *Adult and continuing education in Australia: Issues and practices*. London: Rutledge.

- *Words at work: A report into literacy needs in the workplace* (1991). Canberra: Australian Government Printing Service.

UNIT III
BUILDING THE UNION

Marcus Widenor and Lynn Feekin present a comparative study, this time between the USA and Australia, of developments in "organizing education." Training recruiters is a new important labour education response to the decline of union influence and to shifting employment patterns. Their examination of the AFL-CIO's Organizing Institute and the ACTU's Organising Works allows them to draw conclusions about the relative strengths and weaknesses of the educational and organizational aspects of these central union attempts to boost union recruitment.

France Laurendeau and D'Arcy Martin respond to the challenge issued in Tom Nesbit's chapter for better educational provision for full-time officers (FTOs). They describe a new initiative launched by the Quebec union central Fédération des travailleurs et travailleuses du Québec (FTQ) and argue that this new labour college (Collège FTQ-Fonds) is equipping FTOs with the knowledge and skills to respond to the faster, less certain environment of the globalized economy.

Fernando Lopes illustrates how, in Brazil, *Programa Integrar* (the "integration program" –integrating employment, education and development) offers relevant vocational training and educational opportunities for union leaders as well as employed and unemployed workers. The program responds to both the immediate needs and the future ambitions of the labour movement. Fernando describes how difficult it is to establish union education in a hostile climate but also how ambitious labour education can be in building the union and seeking to change society.

9
Organizer Training in Two Hemispheres: The Experience in the USA and Australia

MARCUS WIDENOR AND LYNN FEEKIN

Dramatic drops in union density throughout most of the western industrial world have prompted national union federations to move more resources into organizing and recruiting new members, a task historically reserved for the affiliated unions of those federations. In many countries, including the United States, Australia, New Zealand and Great Britain, this has led to the creation of new initiatives to recruit and train workplace organizers. [17]

This chapter examines and compares two of these programs, the AFL-CIO's Organizing Institute (OI) and the ACTU's Organising Works (OW). It is based on an examination of documents from both organizations concerning the creation and evolution of the two institutes and on interviews with program administrators and trainees in both countries. After outlining the different origins of the programs and how their attributes are related to specific characteristics of the two national labour regimes, the chapter explores the particular techniques used to recruit and train those organizers. A preliminary investigation indicates new areas for study of the pedagogy of trade union organizer training both in the classroom and in the field and some institutional factors that affect continued organizer effectiveness and whether recruits remain union organizers.

Structural context of the Organizing Institute and Organising Works

The paths to union decline in the United States and Australia have many common origins, including structural labour market changes, technological change, globalization, changed labour laws and weakened enforcement of those laws. However, it is some of the unique differences between the two labour movements that determined the nature of the organizing programs when they were established.

---

[17] There is little critical research on either the AFL-CIO Organization Institute or ACTU Organising Works. Foerster's (2001,) chapter focuses on the internal institutional dynamics that shaped the founding of the program. A more comprehensive research project in Britain, examines the Trade Union Congress Organising Academy established in 1998 (Heery et. al., 2000).

At the heart of those differences is that the US unions have always faced difficulties in organizing due to the representation election process, which initiates the collective bargaining relationship in the US system. Australian unions, on the other hand, enjoyed broad coverage of workers without the threshold of representation elections. One former Industrial Officer for an ACTU affiliate told us: "I was a union staffer for 20 years and never signed up a member." [18] Furthermore, the Australian national system of arbitration awards, established in 1904, meant that wages were more uniform throughout the workforce, reducing the incentive for employers to compete through a non-union wage strategy – a key component of American employer strategies.

The incentive to organize changed drastically for Australian unions in the 1990s when successive reforms of the industrial relations system weakened the coverage of awards, eliminated closed shop agreements, pushed more bargaining to the enterprise level and offered the option of individual worker contracts in lieu of collective agreements. Membership plummeted precipitously over the decade, falling from 50 percent to 30 percent, and Australian unions found themselves in a position similar to that faced by American unions.

In the US, unions had been slowly declining since the early 1950s, and had grappled unsuccessfully with an increasingly hostile labour law system since the passage of the Taft-Hartley Act in 1947. After the failure of labour law reform in the 1970s and 1990s, observers both within and outside the movement increasingly developed a critique of labour's own unwillingness to organize, citing expenditures on organizing at less that 5 percent of most union budgets, as opposed to blaming the external factors that frustrated it.

Increasingly, the re-creation of an "organizing culture" within unions became the focal point for debate of the future of the movement. Organizing became a central issue in the 1995 contested election for top leadership of the AFL-CIO, which Service Employees Union leader John Sweeney won, in part by stressing that the federation would become actively involved in organizing.

Origins of the AFL-CIO Organizing Institute

The Organizing Institute (OI) was established in 1989 by former ACTU strategist Richard Bensinger. The initial program, developed in consultation with organizing directors from various unions and key leadership of the AFL-CIO, was incorporated as an independent corporation outside the structure of the AFL-CIO itself, giving it independence, legitimacy with activist-oriented trade unionists, and the ability to act quickly. The OI's aim was to recruit and provide initial training for a cadre of union organizers. The

---

[18]   Michael Crosby, Director, Trade Union Training Authority. Craft of Organising Training Seminar, Currawong, NSW, 2000.

OI hoped to raise the standards of skills and the status of organizers within their organizations.

But the organizing culture of unions in those early days of the OI was not sufficiently widespread to support adequate "laboratories" for training: "While there was organizing going on in a lot of places, there were very few places that were consistently winning and growing."[19] This prompted the OI in 1992 to convene a task force of elected leadership who would push for a more wide-spread vision of what made for successful organizing.

Structure of the OI Program

The OI was designed as a three-part program, including an initial three-day seminar, a three-week field internship, and finally a three-month apprentice-ship. All 3 components are conducted under the OI auspices, and field trainees and apprentices are paid by the OI. The three-day seminar is based on the practices of various community organizing programs. It was designed to put new organizing trainees through a series of mock exercises focused on crucial components of organizing campaigns, including one on one communi-cation skills, housecalling, organizing committee leadership and campaign planning. All major components of the program use hands-on exercises and mock simulations, with intervening classroom sessions looking at the current crisis of the labour movement and principles of the "organizing" approach to trade unionism.

After a program review by several organizing directors in 1998, the OI's original three-day package was modified to make it more flexible for unions and central labour councils to use. One and two-day versions are now avail-able for unions to use with staff and member organizers on particular campaigns. The OI has custom-designed programs for specific unions, such as a five to ten-day day intensive field training for United Automobile Workers. A Lead Organizer Training program was developed in conjunction with the George Meany Center for Labor Studies and has been offered twice a year since 1999.

Recruitment to the OI

OI trainees come to the program via one of two paths. "Sponsored" partici-pants, usually union members, are recruited by participating unions, while "unsponsored" participants are recruited on college campuses and from com-munity action organizations. From the inception of the program, the OI recruited on college campuses. This effort dovetailed with the AFL-CIO administration's initiatives to raise the profile of the labour movement among young people. In 1996 the AFL-CIO launched its "Union Summer" program,

---

[19]   Allison Porter, interview, November 1999, and communications with the authors, May 2000.

which put 1,000 young people into short summer internship programs. In 1999 Union Summer became a part of the OI.

Between 1990 and 2000 almost 9,000 potential organizers attended the OI's three-day program. The program originally intended to maintain a rough balance of 50/50 sponsored and unsponsored, but rapidly, a majority of trainees coming to the program were sponsored by particular unions. In 1999, when over 1,300 trainees attended the three-day program, 72 percent were sponsored.[20]

There were several reasons for this shift. The OI faced pressure from AFL-CIO affiliates to recruit activists the unions had already identified internally as potential organizers. Some felt that union members should have the first opportunity to participate in the program, while others were skeptical of recruiting students who did not already have some experience in the workplace.[21] The high number of sponsored participants in the three-day program has had repercussions for the continued development of the internship and apprentice stages of the OI. The field components of the program are primarily used by the non-sponsored trainees, while sponsored organizers pursue additional field training largely through their own union rather than the OI.

Who uses the OI?

The first unions to participate in the OI's programs included the steelworkers, food and commercial workers, service workers, clothing and textile workers, and public sector. The communication workers, hotel employees and Teamsters joined soon after. By 1991, 17 unions were participating, representing 80 percent of the total AFL-CIO membership.[22] Requirements for participation include agreeing to send experienced organizers as trainers in the program ("Teaching Fellows") and hosting trainees as interns and apprentices on their campaigns.

Unions have used the program in different ways:

For some unions, the OI was a useful "neutral" mechanism to provide a radical break from the culture of patronage that existed in selecting for staff jobs in the union. For others, it provided a system to test outside candidates before offering them a position. For others, it was a steady source of talent that they didn't have the time to recruit themselves. Initially, all unions experimented with sponsoring members through the training and taking unsponsored candidates on their campaigns. Over time, unions tended to use the program for either training members or recruiting new staff from the outside. Only a few used it for both.[23]

[20] Calculated from OI statistics, AFL-CIO Organizing Institute Program Numbers 1990-1999 (n.d.).

[21] The debate over this issue is reported in Belkin 1996. There was a strong response from some unionists who argued that organizers should have significant prior workplace experience (Early, 1996).

[22] Allison Porter, interview, November 1999, and communications with the authors, May, 2000

[23] ibid.

Three-Day Program Curriculum

The dominant pedagogical feature of the Three-Day program is a series of roleplay exercises where Teaching Fellows (one TF to every three or four trainees) observe and rate the attributes and performance of the participants. In this way the program is actually a screening and selection process rather than a formal training class. It has always been the belief of the OI that real "organizer training" takes place in the field, with affiliates, rather than in a classroom. Nonetheless, some interviewees we spoke to mentioned that they had expected more technical information on the nature of union organizing and development of campaign strategy, and not as much on communications process.

The OI Three-Day Program is organized around four basic themes:
• Organizing is about building relationships and taking action;
• Workers are the union, not a third party;
• Organizing is about issues; and
• Organizing is about power (OI, 1999).

Classroom discussions and exercises are designed to illustrate these key organizing principles in both the strategic and planning aspects of organizing work as well as the one on one communication techniques organizers would use when talking to workers.

In between the exercises, Teaching Fellows rate the trainees on their effectiveness and potential. Early OI programs used written exams and exit interviews with participants in addition to Teaching Fellow observations to rate participants. In 1999 the OI conducted a review of the rating system by 30 lead organizers from various unions, in order to establish uniform criteria throughout the three steps of the program. The result was a list of criteria in four categories: Relational Skills, Leadership and Teamwork Skills, Strategic Ability, and Motivation (OI, 1999). Teaching Fellows are now trained more thoroughly in their assessment skills using the criteria, as well as in the feedback they give participants during the program.

Internship and apprenticeship follow-up

On completion of the three-day program, participants who are rated highly are placed with unions seeking organizers for a supervised field internship. Initially conceived as a three-week program, many AFL-CIO affiliates balked at committing this amount of time to a structured field component. It has now been shortened to a 10-day field exercise, to be followed by a longer, three-month "apprenticeship." In both the 10-day and three-month components trainees are mentored, monitored and assessed by OI staff, in addition to the staff that they may work with from their assigned union.

For the internship, participants are placed on a campaign by a sponsoring union. Regionally based OI field coordinators are assigned to work with the interns on a daily basis. As in the three-day, the field coordinators rate the progress of interns in key areas of the organizing craft. Interns who perform well in the 10-day internship are then placed with a participating union for a three-month apprenticeship. The evaluation of the apprentice's performance is undertaken by the lead organizer, while the OI staff monitors the process and mentors the apprentice when necessary. A common criticism of the OI had been a lack of adequate contact between the OI trackers and apprentices in the field. The OI now provides an organizer skills inventory for participating unions to assist them in mentoring and evaluating trainees.

OI statistics on participation in the field program indicate that 18 percent of all three-day program graduates go on to the internship program, and only 7 percent to the full apprenticeship. The high proportion of sponsored participants who return to their union and therefore don't use the two field components of the OI offers some explanation for these low numbers. The figures are higher for the unsponsored trainees, who utilize the field components more heavily – 31 percent taking part in the internship and 19 percent in the apprenticeship.[24]

The OI has tracked graduates, including the 1993 three-day program trainees. Of a group of 267 they were able to track 77 percent who remained in organizing on a part or full-time basis, while 23 percent had left the labour movement. It is likely that over time the dropout rate is considerably higher (OI, 1993). These figures raise crucial research questions to be addressed in the future.

- Exactly how do trainees make the decision to become union organizers? How long do they stay? What factors affect their decision to remain as organizers?
- What is it that allows people to commit for the long haul, and how do organizers continue to develop their skills and avoid burnout?

Mentoring in the field

Of all the issues we discussed with American and Australian organizer trainees, mentoring was the one they were most adamant about. Whatever their initial experience with the OI or OW, the field training seems most valuable to them if they have a positive mentoring relationship. Unfortunately, this is not always the case. Sometimes the trainee is sponsored by a union whose organizing department is marginalized. Some organizers found themselves assigned solo to campaigns without an experienced lead person in charge. Others found that even when they did have an experienced organizer/supervisor, that person was too far away or too busy to give them the type of feedback they felt they required. The OI's approach to mentoring has become considerably more sophisticated since the beginning of the program, with

---

[24] Calculated from OI statistics, AFL-CIO Organizing Institute Program Numbers 1990-1999 (n.d.).

written guidelines for hosting unions. But these principles can be easily lost in the heat of an organizing campaign where the OI has less and less control over the supervision process.

Organising Works

The Australian Council of Trade Union's (ACTU) created Organising Works (OW) in the early 1990s. Recruitment in Australian workplaces was a relatively passive activity – simply signing up new members, rather than organizing a campaign for union recognition in the workplace as required under American labour law. And since demonstrated workplace strength had no direct effect on the outcome of award arbitrations, the mobilization of members at the workplace, or the running of contract campaigns, was a relatively untested strategy.

OW was established in 1994 after a delegation of Australian officials visited the United States, Canada, Belgium and the UK to investigate different organizing programs. While the delegation understood the concept of the "Organizing Model," they "consciously went in a different direction from the AFL-CIO's Organizing Institute," according to OW director Chris Walton.[25] In 1999 the ACTU further refined its focus on the primacy of organizing, after a second delegation studied organizing programs overseas. This group's report, Unions@Work, summarized a program for renewal of the Australian labour movement inspired by four key principles: Strength in the Workplace, Growth in New Areas, Technology for the Times, and A Strong Union Voice. The organizing philosophy runs throughout the recommendations and is discussed at length in the second section on growth in new areas (ACTU, 1999).

With few lead organizers in the field, OW was forced from its inception to rely more heavily on the classroom component of its curriculum. Due to the lack of indigenous Australian models for organizing activity, the ACTU borrowed heavily from US models. OW is a nine-month program composed of a selection interview process, an initial one-week residential training program and a nine-month period of fieldwork with a union. During the field component, additional residential classroom sessions and follow-up assessment interviews with mentors are also held. Like their American counterparts, OW leaders quickly discovered that the success of the program required transforming organizational structures and priorities within Australian unions.

The need to spread the organizing philosophy more broadly through the leadership of Australian unions led OW and the newly reorganized Trade Union Training Authority (New TUTA) to begin developing training programs and materials for a wider audience than the young recruits attending OW classes. These seminars fulfill the same institutional need as those

---

[25] Phone interview, March, 2000.

sponsored by the OI's Elected Leadership Task Force in the US. Seminars such as Organising in Everything We Do, Planning To Be Effective, Skills of Recruitment and Organising, and the two-week Craft of Organising, are designed for senior union leaders and union staff in order to persuade them to the basic philosophy of the Organizing Model.

The OW was created under the auspices of the ACTU, with top leadership support. The New TUTA became the teaching core of the program, and numerous senior trade unionists were recruited to help organize and participate in the program, giving it wider legitimacy. Chris Walton, an official from the Finance Sector Union, serves as director of the program. The OW's role as a "change agent" is evident from trainees' comments, especially from the early years of the program (1994-96): "They hoped we would go back and help change the union," and "they were preparing us to be the new guard."[26] While we heard some elements of this from American OI participants, the tone in Australia was definitely more urgent and more ideological. Over time the organizing philosophy has become more acceptable in the movement and qualified organizers have more to say about how to actually "do" organizing.

The Organising Works trainees

OW participants are somewhat easier to track than their American OI counterparts. The program is considerable smaller, and most union organizers end up working in one of five main metropolitan areas (Sydney, Melbourne, Brisbane, Adelaide and Perth). Between 1994 and 1998 OW enrolled 284 trainees in six separate intakes and graduated approximately 91 percent of them. An OW survey indicated that in 1998, 65 percent were still employed in the labour movement (Walton, 2000).

While most graduates continued to maintain an organizing focus in their work, only a minority continued primarily as recruiters (Walton, 2000). Many were also doing a substantial amount of traditional servicing work, and some had already moved quickly through the bureaucracy of union and ALP power structures. This backsliding of organizers into primarily servicing roles, which runs counter to the OW's mission, is cause for concern.

In the early years of the program OW graduates tended to be young and predominately from a university or student activist background rather than from the shop floor. For example, in 1995 the largest OW class (132) was predominately female and below the age of 26. This profile began to change in 1996, when the average age rose to 28+ years and fully 70 percent of the trainees were shop floor delegates (Walton, 2000). As in the United States, there was some feeling that the program shouldn't be overpopulated with younger college students without adequate work experience.

---

[26] Interview with Organising Works trainees, Perth, March, 2000.

Recruitment process

The OW sought enrollees not just from ACTU affiliates, but also from among political and community activists, including the Australian Labour Party. Traditionally the ACTU and ALP have enjoyed a closer institutional relationship than the AFL-CIO and Democratic Party's. The ACTU and ALP have served as training grounds for each other's activists.

Generally the recruitment, interviews and screening process of the OW was less rigorous and less systematic than the OI's. Rather than three days of "goldfish bowl" observation of basic organizing scenarios, the OW conducted group interviews to select participants for the initial training group. Interviews took place in small groups, with an OW facilitator asking a series of questions concerning the participants' attitudes towards workers and knowledge of the political and economic context of the industrial relations system. During the interview a small group of observers from the participating unions would focus on the reactions of the trainees. This process seems to have produced a much more competitive environment than that of the OI three-day program.

Organising Works curriculum and field component

The curriculum for the early years of the OW put greater emphasis on the Australia industrial relations system and how unions operate than on the micro skills of member organizing. As the OW has matured, graduates have been brought back to teach in the program. Now that there are more organizers actually practicing the craft, the curriculum has shifted away from the "knowledge based" approach and towards the "skills" of organizing, which now comprise about 80 percent of the curriculum. The OW has clearly evolved more towards the OI model.

One-on-one communication skills form the core of the curriculum, although the contexts used to demonstrate these skills are more likely to be workplace based, rather than the housecall scenario prominent in the OI curriculum. The absence of a predominately "external" organizing terrain in Australia means that many of the strategic questions raised in representation campaigns in the US are not discussed in the OW.

OW graduates who successfully complete the one-week residential program are assigned to unions which have identified preferred recruits during the initial interviewing stage. Field experiences for the Australian trainees vary widely depending on how committed their union is to a long-term strategy of organizing. The OW trainees we spoke to, especially those from the earlier classes, often had a very difficult time once they were in the field. As one put it: "I was like an alien," in a union that "didn't really know what to do with me."[27]

There were very few Australian unionists with enough organizing experience to serve as mentors to OW trainees. Often trainees were assigned to

---

[27] Interview with Organising Works trainee, Perth, March 2000.

Branch Officers who didn't have a clear idea of how to make use of them. A number of Australian trainees felt they should be assigned to non-elected staff so that they were not subject to the internal political intrigues of the union. While some American OI graduates also spoke of the problems of negotiating internal union politics, this was a much stronger complaint among the Australians. Some OW trainees spoke of getting organizing tasks in historically weak organizational centers for union power, which proved to be an insurmountable obstacle for inexperienced organizers. Others describe a general hostile attitude towards the OW program, especially toward young female organizers who were seen as outsiders to the movement.

What probably lay behind the problems many of these organizers faced were unrealistic views of what could be accomplished by novice organizers and an incomplete notion of how to evaluate success. Some unions believed their recruitment rate was the only way to measure whether the organizers were doing a good job, and membership counts became simplistic tools for judgement. This approach ignores the reality that an "organizing culture" requires recruiting more workplace activists and delegating more servicing tasks to members, rather than simply signing up new members. The situation described above has changed as more and more OW graduates have legitimized themselves within Australian unions. In the larger metropolitan areas OW graduates often create their own network for mutual support.

Discussion: Crucial issues facing the OI and OW in comparative perspective

Despite the differences in the American and Australian national labour relations systems, the OI and OW face similar challenges. In their continuing efforts to reverse the dramatic decline of labour's numbers and strength, the OI and OW must confront issues in the following three key areas:

- the relationship between organizer training and the culture of organizing within unions,
- the importance of field training and the mentoring relationship, and
- how to retain organizers over time and ensure that their role remains in organizing.

The first of these – creating a true organizing culture – is a threshold political task that must be confronted if either program is to remain successful. The second two also involve institutional issues, but we are most concerned here with their educational ramifications – how they affect "learning to organize." Here we raise several further research questions that we believe will prove fruitful in enhancing the quality of organizer training.

In today's labour movement, organizing is on everyone's lips. Most union leaders have gotten the message that organizing needs to be the union's number one priority. But in the real world "change to organize" – meaning more resources, more skilled staff, and a strategic organizing plan – is still lacking in many unions. Our research shows that while OI and OW leadership have been acutely aware of this problem, the organizer trainees placed with unions in both countries were sometimes discouraged by their marginalization within the labour movement. We believe this is an even more daunting problem in Australia, where the industrial relations system has been based on the arbitration system for so long. Australian union financial resources are more modest and the structural shifts in labour-management relationships have occurred more rapidly, and are more radical in their implications.

Organizing activity has been sparked within some unions. Unfortunately, neither the magnitude nor the rate of the change has been sufficient to arrest the decline in union density in either country. What is needed is a renewal of commitment to the cultural transformation by the affiliate unions of the AFL-CIO and the ACTU. Without this, the very real progress made by the OI and OW will remain confined to the small group of unions (though large in membership) that have truly committed to transforming their structure and culture to further organizing.

The second area, creating positive experiences in the field and supportive mentoring relationships with senior organizers, is one of the keys to assuring that new organizers learn their craft well. Both programs have made strides in this area, the OI through developing more comprehensive guidelines for monitoring and mentoring trainees in the field, and the OW simply because it now has a cadre of experienced organizers who can serve as mentors. But both programs lose contact somewhat with their trainees once they are working on campaigns.

Another strong component of mentoring has to be a "peer support" network, where trainees have opportunities to continue reflecting with other organizers about their jobs. The OW has set up a series of follow-up classroom sessions for their trainees. Few of the American trainees we spoke with continued to have much contact with their fellow 3-Day participants after they were out in the field.

Finally, organizer burnout is an age-old problem in the US labour movement. While there is little data on the attrition rate for union organizers, we believe it is a crucial issue. We need better information on why people stay organizers, and what it is that makes them leave. Understanding the factors for these decisions, and then addressing them, is critical. Unless we develop a base of senior, experienced organizers who stay in the field, we won't have the mentoring resources to bring in new organizers and teach them what it takes to win.

REFERENCES

- Australian Council of Trade Unions. (1999). *Unions@work: The challenge for unions in creating a just and fair society, Report of the ACTU overseas delegation.* Melbourne: ACTU.
- Belkin, L. (1996, Jan 21). The union kids. *New York Times Magazine.*
- Early, S. (1996). New organizing should be membership-based. *Labor Notes,* April, p.12.
- Foerster, A. (2001). Confronting the dilemmas of organizing: Obstacles and innovations at the AFL-CIO Organizing Institute. In L. Turner, R. Hurd, H. Katz, & R. Hurd, (Eds.), *Rekindling the movement: Labor's quest for relevance in the 21st century.* New York: ILR Press.
- Heery, E. et al. (2000). The TUC's organising academy: An assessment. *Industrial Relations Journal,* 31(5), 400-415.
- Organizing Works. (1993). *Graduate survey, preliminary findings,* Washington: Author/AFL-CIO.
- Organizing Works, (1999, April). *Unions change lives! 3-day training guide for teaching fellows.* Washington: Author.
- Walton, C. (2000, May). *Report to annual general meeting of Organising Works, Inc.* Melbourne: OI.

10

Equipping the Next Wave of Union Leaders: Québec's Collège FTQ-Fonds

FRANCE LAURENDEAU AND D'ARCY MARTIN

"All I know about the phone industry, I learned through my employer. The next wave of union leaders won't have to say that."
René Roy, General secretary, FTQ

This chapter is an initial report on a pilot for training full-time union officers and staff within the Fédération des travailleurs et travailleuses du Québec (FTQ), the largest union central in Québec. It sets out the background for the initiative, explains the context, outlines the objectives and rhythms for the eight-week program, and sketches some implications for labour educators.

The idea of a Québec labour college had been discussed for years. Once they reached the senior level of union activism, the thousand "opinion leaders" within the FTQ felt they had no educational support, that they were on their own. It's not as though trade unionists had never received good union education. On the contrary, at the grassroots level, the FTQ is an educational powerhouse. Hundreds of local union activists are trained as worker educators and lead basic courses within their affiliates on topics ranging from steward training and safety and health to pre-retirement and promotion of French as the language of work. Similarly, those who become involved at any level in community economic development receive sophisticated training through the Solidarity Fund, the labour-sponsored investment fund whose $3.7 billion in assets have spawned an economic education program without parallel in North America. As the most heavily unionized major jurisdiction in the continent, Quebec had developed a substantial labour education system, but within it the FTQ had one gaping hole at the senior level.

This impetus to establish a Quebec labour college was tied intimately to the development of progressive thinking in Quebec nationalism. In the mid-1970s, the FTQ withdrew from the Labour College of Canada, with certain specific concerns about the program and a broader commitment to chart its own path in labour education. During the 1980s, a structure of "sovereignty-association" was put in place whereby the Canadian Labour Congress (CLC) set its own educational priorities and programs, including administration of federal grants in English-speaking Canada, while the FTQ conducted its own affairs autonomously (Gagnon, 1998; Rouillard, 1989).

By the early 1990s, a wider separation of union responsibilities was established whereby the FTQ took over responsibility for issues of union jurisdiction, political action, and other areas that traditionally had been carried by the CLC. At the same time, the Quebec experience in areas including labour-sponsored investment funds and popular education received increasing interest and respect in English-speaking Canada. A defensive, subordinate attitude towards the union experiences of English-speaking Canada was no longer necessary or appropriate. Of course, irritants between the FTQ and CLC remained, but the balance had shifted. One indicator of this shift was the decision by the first director of the Collège FTQ-Fonds, France Laurendeau, to make her first research trip from Montreal to Ottawa, to draw on the experiences of the Labour College of Canada as a starting point for designing the Collège. A second indicator was the decision to involve D'Arcy Martin, a bilingual union educator from Toronto, as part of the initial foursome that comprised the Coordinating Committee that was to design and pilot the program.

The funding for the initiative was a delicate matter, since the Solidarity Fund's Economic Education Foundation had strict limits on the work it could support. Yet the will to support a Collège was clear. At a meeting, the Fund's vice-president Jean Martin asked the four members of the coordination team two questions: "Are you serious this time, so that if we commit funds they will actually be used in this fiscal year?" and: "Can you assure me that the Collège will build collective capacity, and not just enlighten individuals?" These were sobering questions, requiring responsible answers, and they were put by a former local union president whose antennae for empty rhetoric were highly developed. The four members of the Coordinating Committee, along with Jean Sylvestre who took Johanne Deschamp's place after the first session, have struggled to rise to this and other challenges from leaders within the Quebec labour movement.

Context

New initiatives in union education don't occur in a political and economic vacuum. Inside the FTQ, there were four specific triggers for action:

- A new leadership team
- The maturity of the Solidarity Fund as a financial base
- Staff ready to carry out the project
- Linkage to capable and sympathetic university professors.

Let us look at each in turn. At the 1998 convention of the FTQ, a new president, and a new general secretary were elected. Both were personally familiar with FTQ courses and with the struggles and politics of the movement. By that time, the Solidarity Fund of the FTQ had passed $3 billion in assets, with over 400,000 Québecois as shareholders, and mobilized fully 25 percent of the venture capital not just in Quebec but in all of Canada. Both the Education Director and the Research Director had expressed their view to the leadership that it was time to move on the idea of a Collège. Through the protocol established between the Université du Québec à Montréal (UQAM) and the three union centrals, three decades of experience had built trust and mutual respect. As a result, there was no difficulty in establishing an "Academic Committee," with some of Québec's most respected progressive professors in social sciences related to labour issues.

Before the initial program was drafted, the Education Director and the Research Director met for two days with a focus group of union staff to discuss the learning needs of this specific constituency. In addition to working with the committee structure, the Research Director met with a wide range of professors. Officers of the FTQ travelled to Harvard University and to McMaster University to learn from their trade union programs. All the informal channels of input characteristic of the union culture fed into the program development process.

With these conditions in place, adequate supports for learning could be provided. For example, all participants were provided with identical top-quality laptop computers and skilled coaching in using them. The participants in the pilot phase, all union staff, had 75 percent of their salaries reimbursed to the affiliates that employed them, so that replacements could be hired. Thus the two most common excuses for mediocrity in labour education were removed: lack of resources for the educators and lack of time for the participants.

In January 2000 the first group of 13 union staff turned up for the first meeting of the Collège. The eight-week program alternated between time in residence, time at home and time back on the job, spread over a period of six months. At that time, the Collège had no logo, and the name was provisional. The administrative staff person was on a week-by-week contract. The computers were all screwed up. But magic did occur, and the Collège began to earn its place as an incubator for the next generation of union leadership.

Objectives

There was nothing modest in the conception of the Collège. The welcoming words to the first group included:

> Here at the Collège you will be at the leading edge of your knowledge and your capabilities, in order to build the labour movement of the future. You will take a break from the daily grind of union activism to reflect on the needs of our members, of our movement, of our communities. You will have access to good computers, to good food, to good reading material, to good teachers. We have done our best here. This is the maximum of

which we are now capable... We are giving you a beautiful gift: treat it well. Use it to benefit the workers (Rene Roy).

The objectives of the Collège reflect the passionate belief of its initiators in the need to develop capacity to influence the social, economic and political changes underway in Quebec. For this lofty goal to be realized, participants were to be supported in three main areas: knowledge (savoir), method (savoir-faire), and personal/community development (savoir- être).

A sense of how these three objectives are woven into a program might be drawn from the initial outline of the first five days. Day 1 begins with collective discussion of the role of union staff, and the challenges participants experience in that role. In Day 2, the morning involves a lecture on the changing Quebec labour market, while afternoon workshops deal with how to read statistics. Day 3 opens with the politics of unemployment, while afternoon workshops coach people with computers. Day 4 opens with a lecture on community economic development, with the afternoon spent in a historical and political tour of the region where the session is being held. An evening social with family members is followed in Day 5 by a discussion on the stresses of life as a union representative.

"The Collège has been a place to open myself to other ideas, and to develop approaches for the future" (participant comment)

Each evening included "homework" of assigned and optional readings, and each morning opened with a summary of the readings by two participants. Some of the technical texts are challenging, to the point where an improvised workshop was needed on "How to read academic articles!" But a decision was made to expose participants to the best the academy had to offer, and then to support them in drawing on this educational capital effectively. This cannot be done by watering down difficult texts or by facilitating superficial debate.

"Now I understand better how decisions are made around me, and how to analyse situations" (comment of a participant).

In its pilot phase, the Collège's participants have been union staff with a sprinkling of full-time local union officers. Continuing education programs are being designed to keep participants updated on new developments and to strengthen their individual and collective capacity. The first of these, in October 2000, brought Ricardo Petrella of the Lisbon Group to speak on ways of responding to globalization and was followed by workshops related to the People's Summit of the Americas, in Québec City in April of 2001.

Program design

Each participant in the Collège is responsible for a major research project, supported at every stage by individual and collective tutorials. The intent is that they will produce a solid piece of intellectual work, based on their own choice of topic, in a form that can be shared with their families, their colleagues, and the wider labour movement. This is consistent with the FTQ worker educator program, which became a generator of knowledge, not just a transmission belt for the thinking of the leadership. Over time, the Collège should produce original material, at a depth difficult for servicing representatives to achieve in the course of their regular work. Among the topics chosen in the pilot group were:

- The history of labour relations in the Quebec construction industry
- The current situation of Quebec's pulp and paper industry
- The impact of mergers on municipal employees
- Working conditions in private retirement homes
- The pressures on white-collar workers in the manufacturing sector.

These projects embody the "street smarts" of union activism. The process of producing such work has the potential of creating new links between seasoned unionists and the community activists, university professors, statisticians and journalists with whom they come in contact.

"From this experience, I had my personal values questioned, and I got the energy and desire to try new ways of working" (participant comment)

In the Collège, a serious effort has been made to accommodate the rhythms of adult learning amongst working people. The first 10 days in residence include a weekend to which the partners and children of participants are invited free of charge, so that they might better understand and support the climate of learning. This is followed by 10 days at home, during which the participants have specific assignments. While at home, they may access support by teleconference and e-mail, to strengthen study habits in their personal living space.

The first bloc is followed by time back on the job, so that learning can be shared with colleagues and applied in practice. The same rhythm is maintained in the second bloc, so that the seven weeks of intensive work is spread over a reasonable period of time, avoiding what is called "bourrage de crâne" or "stuffing of the brain." After all, the test of success in the Collège is not passing some external exam, but rather equipping people to think, work and live better. This is not helped by cutting people off surgically from working and living. While this distributed rhythm is more costly and less convenient to the affiliates who send participants, it is essential to the human model of learning that underlies the Collège.

"If we are more efficient, we can do more for more people, without burning ourselves out. We can push further in making change." (participant comment)

The first bloc of the Collège takes an economic and historical perspective, while the second bloc takes a social and forward-looking perspective. The workshops of the first bloc are more introductory, while the second bloc works in more depth. Along the way, participants experience alternative processes such as Open Space Technology, and spread their creative wings by selecting and discussing music and art.

Another layer of rhythm is the alternation of popular education approaches, typical of Quebec union education, with academic and corporate tools. The diet is rich, but the process design poses questions and problems and does not indoctrinate people. Role-plays and activity methods are used, but so are formal lectures and the case study methods from the Harvard Business School. The effort of the Collège is to be broad in its sources without compromising its clarity of purpose. Indeed, as a matter of policy, participants are challenged to reflect on their assumptions, rather than simply reinforced in their current convictions.

"I have learned to explore many ways of resolving issues, and to reflect on ways of changing the climate inside unions" (participant comment)

The labour educators

The educators in the College experience a different set of rhythms. Those who start a new labour education program often find it difficult to pass it on to others, or even to make explicit the values and habits with which they have begun. For the four who designed and piloted the Collège, this challenge came quickly, since the success of the first round of courses caused the labour leadership to want greater frequency of sessions, well beyond the capacity of the initial team.

In briefing new members, several assumptions were made explicit, of which the following might be familiar to readers elsewhere with experience in union education teams:

- Spending time on the "personal" among us is necessary and efficient.
- The diversity of learning styles is infinite, and discovering them among participants is our job.
- If participants end up thinking the resource people are intelligent and they are stupid, the program will have failed.
- The responsibility for the Collège lies with the elected leadership of the FTQ and its affiliated unions.

The fourth of the above assumptions is of special significance for the future of the Collège. Here, as in other areas, a key role is played by Michel Blondin, the dean of Québec labour education, now the head of the Economic Education Foundation of the Solidarity Fund and an integral member of the Collège's coordination and facilitation team. Michel was instrumental in establishing, in early 2001, a weeklong program for the FTQ Executive Council to expose them to several of the most effective and provocative resource people. This helped to include the leadership in the learning dynamic to which they assign their staff. In these and other ways, the habits and insights of the Collège are being extended to other parts of union life, and the rhythms of learning sustained beyond the sessions themselves.

Implications

"I'm glad my union sent me here. I feel privileged." (comment of a participant)

After discussion with the "academic committee" of the Collège, university equivalencies were calculated for the program. The total turned out to be well over 250 hours of structured study, with 73 hours of theoretical work, 60 hours of practical skill development, 13 hours of historical and workplace visits and 87 hours of independent supervised study.

For the coordination team, an ongoing evaluation process helped to bring design and facilitation improvements, for the group at hand and for designing the future. This feedback encouraged the team to shift the order of topics and resource people for a more logical flow; to integrate better the theoretical and practical dimensions; to link discussions more to current issues facing the labour movement; to name a few changes.

"The Collège lets you step back from day-to-day union work, to take a fresh approach." (participant comment)

For the participants, regular daily evaluation forms and periodic collective assessments of the program helped to bring together themes; to consolidate learning and to integrate new information and insights; to better transfer knowledge and skill to their roles as full-time union representatives. Of particular importance are the "welcome back" sessions after periods outside the residential setting. Here participants return from their home and work environments, with the "reality checks" of conversation with families, friends and colleagues.

For the union leadership, evaluation is needed to ensure that the considerable investment of money and staff time in the Collège is worth the trouble. After all, an intensive and future-oriented program is bound to cause trouble to the union leadership in the short term. First of all, members and colleagues are likely to complain about the absence of a seasoned union representative for a period of eight weeks; further, the participants return to their union with new ideas and skills, which will de-stabilize their work environment; and finally, a satisfied participant is likely to encourage colleagues to request assignment for future Collège sessions, so that the trouble will be repeated!

The union leadership, who hold in each affiliated union the authority to authorize or withhold participation in the Collège, are a key constituency for evaluation, both informal and formal. They are invited to the closing day of the Collège in order to observe what participants have learned and to question participants publicly and privately about the process and content of the program. Over a longer period, it is these ranking officers of affiliated unions who will see the effects of the Collège on the will, skill and knowledge of their representatives.

What participants learn, and what they say about what they learn, will be the most powerful force in shaping the future of the Collège. In this respect, it is much like the introductory steward courses and the basic health and safety courses that are the bread and butter of labour education. The test of these courses is in whether workers are better represented in their workplaces. When we compare the quality of representation at the leadership level of the FTQ and its affiliated unions a decade from now, the real report card on the Collège can be written.

In this program, the daily practices of union staff are questioned, sometimes reinforced and other times revised or even transformed. The more subtle and long-term effects will be felt in the relation of participants with the membership. In that spirit, we leave the last word to a participant:

> "We can get too caught up in our technical work, and lack the time to think broadly about the labour movement. Yet we're an important link in the union chain. This has restored my energy to push forward, instead of complaining and criticizing all the time. We need to get past a static, mechanical way of working, to keep our militancy, and for that the Collège has been a big help."

REFERENCES

- Blondin, M. (1980). Une formation syndicale faite par les travailleurs eux-mêmes, *Community Development*.

- Blondin, M. (1997). La formation économique des employés, facteur de changement dans les milieux de travail. In *Gestion, Revue des Hautes Études Commerciales*, 22(3), automne.

- Gagnon, M-J., (Ed.). (1998). Un syndicalisme en crise d'Identité. *Sociologie et Sociétés. XXX* (2).

- FTQ. (2000). *Programme d'éducation, 2000-2001*. Montréal: Author.

- Rouillard, J.(1989). *Histoire du syndicalisme québecois*. Montréal: Boréal.

11

Programa Integrar in Brazil: Union Intervention in Employment, Development and Education

FERNANDO AUGUSTO MOREIRA LOPES

Direct union involvement with occupational training in Brazil dates from the 1970s. Vocational schools, for example, were created in the City of São Paulo with funds from international NGOs. These schools were developed, in part, to provide union activists with the skills to enter newly developing industry in Brazil, particularly in steel and metal trades. The 1964 military coup had driven many union activists out of their previous jobs, and left-wing activists, involved in setting up these schools, recognized the importance of attaining vocational qualifications as a way of accessing and organizing the new industries. The union and political work undertaken with some of these trainees had to be clandestine, as the official union leadership had been usurped by the military dictatorship.

In other areas of the country similar initiatives were also carried out. However, over time, occupational training became just one more benefit available to union members, similar to provision of services such as a barbershop, a drugstore and dental assistance.

By the 1980s occupational training was seen as essentially a company responsibility. One government reaction was to revisit the S System – private organizations used to promote sector occupational training and professional development as well as the social well-being of Brazilian workers. This approach to occupational training, which dated back to the Fascist government of the 1940s (SENAI-Industry, SESC-Commerce), was reintroduced in the early 1990s with an additional four sectors covered (including SEST-Transportation and SENAR-Rural). They were funded through employer tax/payroll deductions (between 0.3 percent and 2.5 percent of the total payroll) and with public resources. This system had left a decisive mark on occupational training in Brazil; it has always excluded the involvement of independent unions that have struggled to democratize it for 20 years.

In the 1990s, with the implementation of neo-liberal policies resulting from the process of economic globalization and restructuring of production, profound changes took place, particularly in the manufacturing field. New technologies and management techniques for involving the worker were implemented. Along with an increase in the physical demands of the job there were added psychological burdens due to an accumulation of functions and the requirement to "wear the company shirt" (to always act and think corporation) in search of greater competitiveness.

High unemployment aided entrepreneurs in eliminating any possibility of resistance. Production "islands" replaced assembly lines, the floor was coloured blue, and machines and operators were coloured white. Flexibility, workplace learning, the ability to work in teams, to make decisions, to communicate, and to be independent were the occupational requirements of the new worker. These qualities were imposed in the majority of cases more as a way to select and eliminate positions rather than as a real requirement for efficiently performed work.

Given the country's size and the disparity in development levels of its various regions, a traditional model of work organization persisted. In these locations production processes follow along the lines of the Ford-Taylor model. But even though it is still possible to produce according to the Ford-Taylor model, the tendency is to follow the new management techniques described in the paragraph above.

These changes weakened the traditional systems of occupational training, based on trades training. The government imposed a reform of technical education, a new model called Certification of Skills and a new classification of the Brazilian Occupational Register (CBO). These reforms were similar to developments elsewhere, particularly in Australia and Britain.

At the local union level, workers concerned with these transformations began to place occupational training on their list of priorities. At its 7th National Plenary Session, the Unified Central Labour Union (CUT) brought together resolutions from its earlier congresses and plenary sessions and established a body of resolutions on this subject, reaffirming the need for a new type of institution to manage occupational training programs, Public Occupational Training Centres.

In September 1995, the Third CNM/CUT (National Confederation of Metalworkers of the Unified Central Labour Union) Congress was held, at which a resolution was passed making occupational training part of the union agenda. It became a goal to be negotiated with every company. The resolution defined conceptual guidelines and initiated the development and implementation of a CNM/CUT pilot project. The project was to be a part of the metalworkers' action strategy, fighting against the neo-liberal policies through purposeful resistance and the struggle over hegemonic ideas. This political action was carried out in two directions:

- Participation in general social struggles and intervention in public policies;

- Organizing the national union.[28]

In consequence, *Programa Integrar* (the Integration Program) was formed as part of the political action within the metalworkers' overall action strategy. This meant that it was not just a "scholarly experiment" but was linked to CNM/CUT's National Training Secretariat, incorporating the union's training objectives into its curriculum and methods. The implementation of the program is the responsibility of the affiliated unions and is integrated into local union activities.

For the project to satisfy CNM's strategy of struggling for hegemonic influence it was necessary to work with three distinct groups: union leaders, employed workers and unemployed workers.

The Integration Program for the Training of Union Leaders (PIFD)

CUT had already a rich experience in union training for union leaders, which needed to be reworked to overcome shortcomings. This being the case, the Leaders' Training Program became a regular course in 2000, with an integrated curriculum, where specific knowledge of the union area was linked to general knowledge at the elementary and secondary education levels.[29] The objective here was to train union leaders to meet the challenges that face the movement today. The program is structured as follows:

(a) A monthly activity, programmed in eight modules, that is, four units of 48 hours each, organized in two 24-hour modules. These units deal in an interdisciplinary structure with elementary and secondary education, linked to themes such as Transformations in the World of Work, Union Activity, Union Organization, and Active Citizenship;

(b) A fan-out process (planned activity) as a complement to training, where each of the regular students takes on the commitment to meet with at least 10 leaders or basic activists on a monthly basis, between two of the course's modules, performing a planned, related activity lasting eight hours;

These meetings prepare the union leaders through organizing activities, speeches, exhibitions, and debating with other workers in their factory or group of factories for which they are responsible. The idea is to place a worker in a practical task, to pass on knowledge, to discuss, to set a direction and, in particular, to convince other workers to support the union's ideas;

---

[28]   In Brazil a fascist union model is still strong dating from the fascist governments of Getulio Vargas (dating from the 1930s to 1954) promotion of "capital-oriented" unions, hindering the organization of a national "labour-oriented" union.

[29]   These two levels comprise 11 years.

(c) A process of reflection in which each group of participants reflects, studies, and plans and evaluates an activity at least once a
week for four hours. This activity eventually will include a
trainer, who will accompany and direct the study circle;

(d) Programmed participation in other planned training activities,
offered by CUT as well as CNM, or through international cooperation agreements;

(e) An individual study course (Individual Study Plan) through
which participants can deepen their knowledge of specific topics
related to their union practice;

(f) Complementary learning, as part of the participants' commitment to study a foreign language or computers; and

(g) A levelling process in basic Portuguese and mathematics. With
their own resources and the help of the trainer, participants will
be able to improve their knowledge of mathematics and Portuguese (conditional activities).

Rather than a mere course, this is an integrated qualification program for
union leaders, in which participants will act as advisers or leaders in debates
on a given topic. Within one year, at least 15,000 union leaders will be able to
participate in CNM's training process. At the time of writing, 500 leaders are
taking this program, which will provide certification at the elementary and
secondary school levels, and a further group of 56 leaders will complete an
extension course in Labour Economics at the Faculty of Economics of
Campinas University (UNICAMP), preparing for an undergraduate course at
the same university.

The Integration Program for the Employed (PIE)

For employed workers, an earlier discussion with COPPE/UFRJ[30] was
revisited, and an attempt was made to negotiate direct occupational training in
companies, beginning with a survey and other participatory research. The survey was carried out in 10 companies, and the privately published reports of
them are now available. The research results assisted in shaping the Integration Program for the Employed (PIE), composed of three connected
subprograms:

(a) Basic Training, integrating areas of elementary and secondary
school knowledge;

(b) General Technical Training, focusing on recent technological
changes in the company's productive sector; and

---

[30] Coordination of Research and Graduate Studies at the Federal University of Rio de Janeiro.

(c) Focused Technical Training, aimed at meeting the needs of a given company segment or position.

The Integration Program for the Unemployed (PID)

After the Congress, CNM/CUT carried out a survey through informal conversational groups in Largo 13 de Mayo, São Paulo, where there is a large concentration of unemployed workers. Based on the discussion and classification of this survey, CNM/CUT produced a draft program with five technical areas (Work and Technology, 120 hrs; Mathematics 180 hrs; Reading and Interpreting Drawings, 120 hrs; Management and Planning, 120 hrs; and Computers, 160 hrs) organized into 13 modules. Unemployed workers can continue to accumulate credits, so that if there should be a need to interrupt the program because of work, they will have a certificate for the module they have finished and can later resume their courses and complete the modules they are missing.

The CNM/CUT project faced the challenge of organizing the content in various areas around the concrete reality of the changes in work and society, linking and revealing the connections, and so allowing the students to gain a historical understanding. The Integration Program for the Unemployed was conceived to be political action – as part of a union strategy by and for unemployed workers. The program goes beyond the limits of a strictly educational project. It is configured as an alternative, more holistic, public employment policy, differentiating itself from and opposing the policy implemented by government bodies.

For CNM/CUT, it is important that PID regain the "public" feeling. That is, rather than restricting itself to what the government is doing, it aims to involve all of society, taking into consideration all the dimensions of the unemployment problem, and focusing on collective action by the unemployed, the main subject of this project, in the search for alternatives.

Towards these aims, CNM/CUT is proposing a training program that takes into consideration the development of cognitive skills, that is, a capacity to reason, communicate, elaborate, make abstractions and plan. Because they are equally important, social skills are also incorporated, such as decision-making ability, working as part of a group, showing independence, respecting differing opinions and, above all, expressing solidarity. These skills and abilities are requirements for reintegration into the modern productive process and for income-generating activities and are the essential prerequisite for exercising active citizenship.

In accordance with the instrumental point of view, so highly valued in the traditional occupational training culture, the Integration Program uses computers for its training. Computers are regarded as the basis for all the technological transformations in progress, and are an indispensable tool for any type of work and for learning that uses global communication systems.

With computer training, linked to improved education, the CNM/CUT project opens up a fairly broad range of work opportunities, extending further but costing less than traditional courses using traditional learning methods. Beyond this, the speed with which technological innovations, equipment, new materials and different ideas are being implemented makes it impractical to offer a collection of traditional fragmented courses which would be rapidly outdated by new changes.

Joint Sustained Development Laboratories (LDSS)

This support program was established as part of PID. It examines alternative ways of generating income for participants. In this regard, economic solidarity must be understood as another instrument of action, of organization of workers and in particular of the unemployed, and one which provides a political and collective orientation to their income-generating activities. LDSS consequently seek answers to the following questions:

- Is economic solidarity possible?

- Are cooperatives the only form of joint enterprise?

- Are joint enterprises viable without at least being linked to a local development plan?

- Is local development possible in the context of the neo-liberal policy?

- What does a local development plan consist of and what volume of resources is required to make it viable?

- What institutional arm would create it and how can its predominance be guaranteed?

- How can success be ensured, and how can the values inherent in solidarity be realized?

LDSS, is much more than an alternative response to unemployment, and raises questions whose relevance makes the program fundamental among all the activities developed by the Integration Program. Therefore, LDSS has taken on the intervener's role, i.e., that of establishing a new platform for joint undertakings, allowing the isolated, compartmentalized initiatives to gain strength. In this way, alternatives have been discovered for generating income, linking that to new models of organization and making them viable. This intervention is deployed through three activities:

1. Linking: involving local institutions, resulting in the setting up of a Local Development Forum;

2. Mapping out the local reality: institutions, social movements, public policy priorities, local and regional economic potential, and researching and analyzing projects under study and being implemented; and

3. Developing projects based on the workers' perspective.

The Local Development Forum has been very well received by all segments of society, particularly the city councils. The mapping indicates that social movements already have projects in line with their interests and see a strong possibility of mobilizing and accessing public resources from other legitimate sources for their projects. In this way, LDSS, founded on union action, is mobilizing the social movements and their allies and building them from a workers' perspective.

Curriculum and methods

The programs prepare participants for work with methods and curriculum based on a concept of education that assists learners to be creative, critical and has a capacity to intervene in social processes. Participants are considered active citizens who build social relationships that help establish society within the concrete conditions of the historical moment.

Knowledge is seen as the result of a constructive process. It does not spring from a mere accumulation of information. The learners bring their real experiences to the learning process. This philosophy gives direction to the actions of students, educators, the curricular structure and educational activities.

The student's knowledge and its integration in the education process

In the Local Development Forums, worker-students are considered individuals whose cognitive, physical, emotional, economic, political, social, cultural, ethical, aesthetic and spiritual dimensions interact in the process of building knowledge. The accumulated knowledge of adult workers is fundamental to the methodology and serves as a starting point, which is then broadened and systematized. It is important to emphasize that this work-based and community knowledge, accumulated by the students throughout their working lives, is the raw material from which new knowledge is developed. Starting with the life experiences and knowledge brought by learners, educators became animators of processes that can modify both learners' and teachers' knowledge, as well as broaden the students' capacity to intervene in the society in which they live.

The structure of the curriculum

The programs have an integrated structure, with the worker-student's learning situated in the scenario of the world of work, the transformations that world is undergoing, and the life and academic experiences of that worker-student. The curriculum links the knowledge of technical areas to general knowledge. The selection of the technical area is related to the worker's experience and to job opportunities. The goal is to assist individuals with new skills including the ability to make complex decisions. In this regard, the approach is based on understanding the knowledge related to these areas, and not on training directed only at operating and managing equipment. The technical areas include knowledge of Productive Restructuring, Mathematics, Control of Measurements, Reading and Interpreting Drawings, and Computers.

The inclusion of general knowledge in the curriculum stems from a concept of education that rejects the limitations imposed by traditional occupational training practices. The objective is to train a worker who appropriates culture and human knowledge and who understands technical matters, science and culture as parts of a single reality. This knowledge includes the Portuguese language, History, Geography, English, Mathematics, Biology, Physics and Chemistry (contents worked out in an integrated process which incorporates technical knowledge).

Educational activities

Linking of students' everyday reality to the various areas of knowledge leads to the question of initiating action. Based on the relationship established among the various program levels, concepts and values are given new significance, making it possible to initiate collective actions.

Collective action, through educational workshops and seminars, are ideal for linking education and work. Based on the necessities pointed out by the students, the research carried out and the discussions raised in the classroom, it is in educational workshops that the students, the community and institutions discuss collective alternatives for generating employment and income and sustainable human development policies.

The educational workshops are directed at the community and are intended to involve participants from local institutions: municipal councils, municipal employment commissions, groups in civil society, the legislative power, small companies, local unions, etc. These workshops stress employment and income generation and sustainable human development, with a view to identifying alternatives to unemployment.

The educational seminars also propose to broaden students' perspectives through visits to museums, factories, exhibitions and experiences in the areas of painting, dancing, music, literature, science fairs, etc. Such activities are intimately related to classroom work, planned with the students and evaluated afterwards.

The evaluation process

The Integration Program practices an evaluation that follows the quality of the teaching-learning process and enables participants to engage in continuous reflective activity. Evaluation is continuous, diagnostic and process-related and guides the daily classroom planning through analysis of the student's difficulties and progress as well as evaluation of the trainer's work. Evaluation is conducted using various instruments and takes into consideration the context and participation of the student, group and educators.

Political action

The Integration Program enables students to take a critical view of social problems. This educational action is part of a larger front that includes the popular democratic political parties, organizations of civil society and union movements, with the goal of changing the economic policy of the country.

Conclusion

CNM/CUT's strategy of "purposeful resistance and discussion of hegemony" means opposition to the deleterious effects of neo-liberal policies, with proposals to overcome them and a discussion of ideas aimed at designing a new society where social inclusiveness, democracy, and respect for human beings and nature would be permanently pursued. In this context, the development of the *Programa Integrar* allows us to occupy places in society, whether in association with NGOs and public institutions or as unions on the factory floor. The development of strategic actions such as participative research increases workers' power over the productive process, equipping them to fight for control over the pace and manner of manufacturing goods and products that are to be made available to all.

Programa Integrar, and union and occupational training in general, is meant as a training tool for political action for leaders and employed and unemployed workers for a process of real action in society. In Brazil we understand that education and training is not an end in itself. But by coming together in training programs we are also increasing union militancy and producing a more qualified leadership and therefore creating the conditions for progress.

UNIT IV
CURRENT CHALLENGES

This section opens with a fascinating and detailed study by Doug Miller of the measures taken and the progress made by European trade unions to equip their members with the skills, knowledge and confidence to represent members' interests on corporate European Works Councils. This is clearly an extension of core labour education – representative training – but at a level at which unions have not been represented previously. The ambiguities surrounding the legislation are matched by those of the "location" in which European Works Councilors find themselves as they move from "place" to "space."

Keith Forrester reports on union involvement in workplace learning in the UK. Some of the evidence flowing from union activity in workplace learning is contradictory and there has been a growing recognition by those involved of the problematic nature of union-workplace learning initiatives. Keith argues for a union definition of workplace learning and notes the important contributions of UNISON amongst others to the debate and practice of workplace learning. He also discusses the progress made with the idea of workplace-based "learning representatives," an idea that could have universal applicability.

Jeffery Taylor describes the pioneering developments in union on-line learning that he has been involved with in Canada. He documents how unions have responded to the educational challenges posed by widespread computer use and the Internet and explains the uses made of a solidarity network (SoliNet) in Canada in the early 1990s and the more recent examples of e-learning. He argues for a continuing investigation of the uses of on-line education for union members in the new century and that there is an obvious use for labour on-line learning in building education across national boundaries.

12

Training Transnational Worker Representatives: The European Works Councils

DOUG MILLER

Developments within the global economy in the final decade of the last century have seen significant changes in the response of organized labour to the mobility of multinational capital. The challenge for trade unions has been to break the insularity of labour as the occupant of "place" and to emulate capital as the occupier of "space" (Wills, 1998). Events in Europe in the mid 1990s have the potential to change this situation[31]. A statutory instrument known as Directive 94/45/EC on Information and Consultation in Community Wide Undertakings – issued in 1994 – obliged some 1,200 eligible multinational corporations (MNCs) in the European Economic Area (EEA) to negotiate information disclosure and consultation procedures with their employee representatives. For the first time lay workplace representatives from the countries in which those MNCs have operations were given the opportunity to meet with their counterparts and face their central European management to discuss the implications of their company's strategy. The Directive applies to all companies, including those with corporate headquarters outside the EEA, that have more than 1,000 employees in at least two EEA States, and where there are a minimum of 150 workers at each of two plants. It was to be translated into national law by September 1996 and, in the two-year transition period, companies were free to negotiate voluntary "Article 13" agreements and set up their own procedures. Between September 1996 and September 1999 companies were expected to have reached agreement on the basis of the requirements of the Directive under the terms of the respective national law that transposed the Directive. By 1999 formal meetings of EWCs have taken place in over 7000 of 1200 eligible MNCs (EWC, 1999). It is estimated that by the time the process of negotiation is complete some 15 million workers will be represented by in excess of some 25,000 new transnational representatives. For the first time transnational representation has been given a degree of structure and permanence as MNCs have been obliged to cede "space" to their employee representatives.

---

[31] This is not to diminish the significance of embryonic forms of European wide collective bargaining (Marginson & Sisson, 1998), principally between the European employers' association UNICE and the European trade union confederation ETUC, and the establishment of links between trade union movements in Western, Central and Eastern Europe

This occupation of "space" has not been emerging spontaneously and organically as a logical extension of worker organization. The long march to employee representation in MNCs was led very much by a Brussels based European trade union bureaucracy (Hall, 1992). What this chapter is particularly concerned about is the way in which organized labour has risen to the enormous technical and political challenges posed by the Directive. Technical, because the process of preparing for, negotiating and operating within a so-called European Works Council (EWC) calls for new areas of knowledge, new skills and new perspectives on the part of employee representatives. Political, because, as we shall see, the peculiarity of the European Works Council presents some very real obstacles to the development of cohesion among worker representatives at this level (Ramsay, 1997, p. 522-525; Wills, 2000). Reflecting on the pedagogical response to these challenges may yield some lessons for the development of transnational trade union education in the future. In this chapter some of the pedagogical issues confronting trainers are briefly discussed before observations for transnational trade union education are offered in the conclusion.

EWC training: The context

It is necessary at the outset to critically assess the parameters within which EWC representatives are likely to have to operate. The first concerns the rights afforded to representatives in the EWC Directive that extend only to the provision of limited information and consultation.[32] Despite such limitations there is evidence of some EWCs being able to push out the boundaries of their jurisdiction to cover health and safety, equal opportunities, vocational training and labour standards, and to engage in productive dialogue on these issues (Marginson & Sisson, 1998).

It is much too early to speculate about possible future bargaining roles for such bodies. There is not only major resistance from the multinationals themselves but also critical distance taken within the European trade union movement fearful of the impact of "company egotism" on sectoral bargaining (Moody, 1997, p. 245-6). Secondly, in the annual information meetings with the central European management of an MNC, which form the focal point of the Directive, EWC representatives are likely to be confronted with a "dislocating" experience (Edwards & Usher, 1997). The requirement to cope with often quite different national information systems and accounting conventions as well as distinctive systems of workplace representation, coupled with immediate problems of communication, language and cultural difference provide

---

[32] The absence of any "bite" in the Directive was demonstrated most forcibly with the decision by Renault to unilaterally close the Villevorde plant in Belgium in advance of the annual meeting with the EWC. In contrast to those national works council systems common in much of the EEA, EWCs have been afforded no statutory rights in relation to consultation or participation in decision making, leading Streeck (1997) to conclude that the title "works council" is already a misnomer.

for a disorienting mix. Such dislocation is not helped by an absence of any debate about what it means to be a "European" works councillor (Miller, 1999), so that worker representatives may lack guidance in moving from a national to a transnational perspective.

Third, it is by no means guaranteed that new works councillors will be experienced representatives, or that experienced representatives will find their way and/or enjoy competent organizational support where they are unionized. The picture is further muddied by composition formulae on European Works Councils, which provide for a complex and complicating mix of occupational, sectoral, and national cultures and of different cultures of trade unionism and non-unionism. In addition many EWCs operate within conglomerates, where the interests are often too diverse for there to be meaningful dialogue among the delegates and between the delegates and management.

Significantly, the EWC Directive rests on the principle of employee versus trade union representation (there is no explicit mention of trade unions whatsoever in the Directive). This can provide for curious compositions on an EWC, with not only non-union representatives but also senior managers as workforce "delegates."[33] Consequently any EWC may have forces pulling at it in four directions – those internal to each EWC (formal and informal co-operation among EWC members), those vis-à-vis management; those in relation to national structures of employee representation; and finally those prevailing between the EWC and the trade unions (Lecher et al., 1997). In addition and somewhat unsurprisingly, transnational representation has replicated the gender inequalities present in national trade union structures (Cockburn, 1996). The jockeying for a favourable position within the Single European Market has intensified the process of concentration, merger and takeover (Edwards, 1999) so that it is not uncommon for newly elected EWCs to find themselves under new ownership and in need of re-constitution. The upshot of such a complex array of factors means that no two European works councils can ever be the same. This is of crucial importance in the delivery of training and a point to which we must return later.

The training infrastructure

Rights to training

Given the vagaries within the context of this new tier of industrial relations, one might have expected the drafters of the Directive to include a specific right to training.[34] Only the Netherlands included specific provision for

---

[33]   Nevertheless trade unions have been able to dominate EWC negotiations in the first wave of Article 13 agreements and have by and large successfully organized to ensure trade union representation. In some cases this is by default since many employee representatives, who are from member states where works councils rather than trade unions are the preferred form of workplace representation, are de facto trade union representatives. In other cases trade union presence may be guaranteed in the person of a coordinator/expert who is permitted to take part in the pre-meeting and formal meeting with management.

training in its transposition of the Directive into Article 4 of its 1996 European Works Council Act. This leaves trade unionists in other countries relying on an uneven pattern of legal rights commonly formulated in the 1970s and subject to interpretation in relation to EWCs (Stirling & Miller, 1998). The absence of a steer in the Directive has resulted in a differentiated and uneven infrastructure and pattern of training provision. Of course, some European Works Council agreements themselves have included specific reference to training, and detailed analysis has shown that between approximately one fifth and one third of agreements specifically do so (Marginson et al., 1998 Miller & Stirling, 1998). Agreements themselves are not the only measure of training provision, nor do they necessarily give an indication of employers' attitudes. However, the situation is serious enough for training to be an item on the agenda for the upcoming revision of the Directive (Buschack, 1999) and the European Industry Federations (EIFs) (the regional bodies of the International Trade Secretariats) have made such provisions explicit in their guidelines for negotiators of EWC agreements.

Providing bodies

For much of the preliminary phase of establishing EWCs the bulk of training provision for European works councillors was heavily dependent on start-up funding from the European Commission. This financial infrastructure or budget line, known as B3-4004/3, was set at 14 million ECU for its first year of operation in 1992. Each year up to the transposition of the Directive in 1996 the fund supported structured exchanges and preparatory meetings between worker representatives pending the introduction of European-wide systems of information and consultation. These had a significant training content and were coordinated in the first instance by the EIFs and then by the European Trade Union College – a peripatetic providing body that appointed a designated EWC training officer in 1994 with a remit to organize and implement sectoral, inter-company and company-based seminars on behalf of the EIFs (Miller & Stirling, 1998). Below the European level, the national confederations have had varying degrees of involvement in EWC training provision. This has included assisting in the coordination of multi-union applications to the budget line; organizing periodic conferences to review issues relating to the implementation of the Directive and applying for funds themselves as organizers and providing bodies (as, for example, in the cases of the British TUC, German DGB, the Dutch FNV, the Danish LO and the Italian CISL). Some national affiliates of the EIFs, such as the British TGWU and the German IG Metall, consider transnational information and consultation so important that they have devoted significant resources to establishing their

---

[34] The subsidiary requirements established in Point 7 of the Annex to the Directive only state that "the central management concerned shall provide the members of the European Works Council with such financial and material resources as enable them to perform their duties in an appropriate manner."

own national EWC training and organizing units. Providers have been swift to realise the need for transnational teams of trainers to deliver the training and this itself has generated new training needs on the part of trade union educators (ETUCO/AFFET, 2000)

Approaches to curriculum

Because trade unions have been entering uncharted territory, curriculum has evolved somewhat organically and pragmatically. Nevertheless course and content design has been occurring collaboratively between national centres, often aided by Commission funding and assisted by the European Trade Union College (for a list of projects, see www.etuco.org/etuco/en/projects/) Given the multi-faceted context of any given EWC it is likely erroneous to be too prescriptive on course content. Recent work has developed models of training needs analysis, which may assist individual EWCs in determining their training agendas (Miller, 2001). More generic training needs analysis has concluded that there is a set of core representational skills, which EWC representatives are likely to require as a prerequisite, (TUC, 2000 – Leonardo curriculum guidelines).[35] Since such core representational skills are transferable, it is likely that training can be delivered at the less costly national level for some delegates. Beyond this the formal management information events and the pre-meetings between representatives have thrown up five key areas of curriculum that have been confirmed in successive training needs analyses (Buchholz, 1998; ETUCO, 1998; Miller, 2001). Whilst the first two – reading and interpreting accounts, data handling and the development of information and communication strategies – arguably are familiar territory in national trade union education curricula, three new areas have emerged that are germane to this level of representation: *language competence, cultural awareness* and *comparative industrial relations*. It is this transnational curriculum that presents trainers with considerable pedagogical challenges.

Cultural awareness, for example, is a particularly problematic area. Companies have supported training in this area, since it may be an opportunity for them to place emphasis on what divides rather than unites workers. Yet it embraces the full gamut of what has come to be termed "social" competences (Rehbock, 1994): conflict resolution, inter-personal communication, gender[36] and multicultural awareness and team-building. Effective training here needs to be group-specific and run at the level of the full EWC. Yet these are areas of trade union education that have only fairly recently taken a more prominent yet still marginal place within national training programs, and for which techniques, particularly in a multi-lingual and multi-cultural context, are still in their infancy. Trainers in this area need to be not only highly socially skilled (and ideally multi-lingual) but also

---

[35] It cannot always be assumed that every EWC delegate will be versed in basic skills of note taking, report writing, and public speaking .

[36] Attempts are being undertaken to "mainstream" gender in transnational training (CISL, 1998).

knowledgeable about the issues affecting workers as well as the differing approaches to industrial relations within the EEA. Unfortunately, many trainers who are skilled in this area have cut their teeth in management development rather than trade union education.

Methods

The particular operational constraints of EWCs do present trainers with considerable methodological challenges. Methodological innovation may be constrained by three critical factors: *cost, interpreting* and *the use of experts.*

An average EWC training event is likely to run between two and five days. They may precede the formal EWC meeting. Such events are often the main recurring cost for employers (ECOTEC, 1999). Funding and the basis upon which it is administered can be of crucial importance in determining pedagogical content and method and mode of delivery. There is a range of possible funding models (Miller, 1999) as we move to a revision of the Directive, but trade union proposals on training are not explicit about the issue (Buschack, 1999). Some EIFs, e.g. the European Building and Woodworkers Federation, are keen, for instance, on the establishment of a clear budget for EWCs. Related to the issue of cost is the key expenditure involved in interpreting and translation, arguably the most important precondition for effective communication between worker representatives. Some agreements appear to treat language training as a substitute for interpreting and translation, in a context where many MNCs have made English their working language (Miller et. al., 2000). Putting aside the issue of anglo-centrism, this has two major impacts on method. First, if interpreting resources are constrained, this can restrict the degree of small-group work, which can predispose an event towards an expert-centred approach. Secondly, often for reasons of time or management resistance, there is a paucity of tailored training materials in the necessary languages. Consequently trainers have to consider visualization as a key method. However, when the latter method was used in several training events, some participants felt patronised.

Conclusion: Towards a pedagogy for transnationality?

To what extent does the European experience offer any insights for trade unionists elsewhere? First, the development of transnational worker organization through EWCs has demonstrated that representatives at this level acquire a new range of skills which in turn have opened up some entirely new fields for trade union education. However, like any other substantive issue in labour education, these are fields that require not only worker/trade union control, but also a systematic rather than ad hoc approach on the part of labour educators. Secondly, the pattern of national trade union legislation and training provision is so varied that it cannot provide a reliable basis for the new transnational training necessary in a global context. What is unavoidable is that those issues that can in some way be addressed by training will at best be addressed in a training event organized by and for the whole European Works Council. For the first time the development of EWCs provides an opportunity to apply the benefits of the concept of the "learning organization" (Fenwick, 1998, p.140) to a trade union education context. But because trade union control over content and method can at best be only indirectly assured, there is a risk that the EWC becomes "tied to the bumper of the overall company direction controlled by management" (Fenwick, 1998, p. 147). Consequently the task for organized labour, where it has a foothold in those EWCs that have been constituted, is to ensure that the training agenda is determined in a democratic and transparent manner. Fortunately, because of traditions prevailing in Europe that have historically ensured a trade union presence in systems of employee (rather than trade union) representation,[37] a networked trade union infrastructure is emerging to support EWCs in this task. Significantly, however, this somewhat haphazard infrastructure could not have emerged without the financial support of a supranational European Parliament and Commission with the appropriate political will.

REFERENCES

- Buchholz K. (1999). Internationale bildungsarbeit – eine Herausforderung fuer die Gewerkschaften. *Arbeit und Politik* (26), 41-47
- Buschack W. (1999). Five years after: A look forward to the revision of the EWC Directive. *Transfer* 5(3), 384-392.
- Cockburn, C. (1995). Women's access to European industrial relations. *European Journal of Industrial Relations* 1(2), 171-89.
- Edwards, R. & Usher, R. (1997). Globalization and a pedagogy of (dis)location. *Proceedings of the 27th Annual SCUTREA Conference*, University of London: 136-140.
- Edwards, T. (1999). Cross border mergers and acquisitions: The implications for Labour. *Transfer* 5(3), 320-344.
- ETUCO. (1997). *Enquiry on training needs of workers' representatives in European works councils.* Brussels: ETUCO.
- ETUCO. (1999). *Costs and benefits of European Works Councils.* London: Dept. of Trade and Industry.
- European Works Council. (1999). Article 6 state of play. *Bulletin 22,* July Aug. 10-15.
- Fenwick, T. (1998). Questioning the concept of the learning organization. In S. Scott, B. Spencer, & A.M. Thomas (Eds.), *Learning for life: Canadian readings in adult education* (pp.140-152). Toronto: Thomson Educational Publishing.
- Hall, M. (1992). Behind the European Works Council directive: the Commission's legislative strategy. *British Journal of Industrial Relations* 30(4), 547-66.

---

[37]   Often via an explicit role for trade unions in the training of employee representatives (Stirling & Miller, 1998).

- Lecher W., Nagel B., Platzer H.W. (1997). *The development of European Works Councils from information committee to social actor.* Düsseldorf : WSI.

- Marginson P., Gilman M., Jacobi O. & Krieger, H. (1998). *Negotiating European Works Councils: An analysis of agreements under Article 13.* Brussels: European Foundation for the Improvement of Living and Working Conditions and the European Commission, Interim Version, March.

- Marginson P. & Sisson, K. (1998). European collective bargaining: A virtual prospect ? *Journal of Common Market Studies, 36*(4), 505-528.

- Miller, D. (2001). Transnational worker representation and transnational training needs: The case of European Works Councils. *International Journal of Training and Development, 5*(1).

- Miller, D., Tully, B. & Fitzgerald, I. (2000). The politics of language and European Works Councils : Towards a research agenda. *EJIR.* November.

- Miller, D. (1999). Towards a European Works Council. *Transfer,* Brussels ETUI 5(3), 344-365.

- Miller, D. and Stirling, J. (1998). European Works Council training – An opportunity missed? *European Journal of Industrial Relations, 4*(1), 35-56.

- Moody, K. (1997). *Workers in a lean world.* London:Verso.

- Ramsay, H. (1997). Solidarity at last ? International trade unionism approaching the millennium. *Economic and Industrial Democracy, 18,* 503-537.

- Rehbock A. (1994). Bildung be-greifen. Soziale Kompetenz als didaktische Grundlage in der Qualifizierung von ehren-und hauptamtlichen Funktionsträgern. In J. Richert (Ed.), *Subjekt und Organization.* Münster: Westfälisches Dampfboot.

- Stirling, J.& Miller, D. (1998). Training European trade unionists, *International Journal of Training and Development, 2*(2), 108-118.

- Streeck, W. (1997). Neither European nor Works Councils: A reply to Paul Knutsen. *Economic and Industrial Democracy, 18,* 325-337.

- Wills, J. (1998). Uprooting tradition: Rethinking the place and space of labour organization. *European Planning Studies, 6*(1), 31-42.

- Wills, J. (2000). *Great expectations: Three years in the life of an EWC.* (Paper number 5. Department of Geography). London: University of London.

13

Unions and Workplace Learning: The British Experience

KEITH FORRESTER

ny analysis of trade union activity, as it emerges into the 21st century, is likely to be situated within a framework that lists the problems and difficulties confronting organized labour. Given the intimacy with which trade unions are historically woven into their socio-economic environment, the focus on problems (and even crisis) is not surprising. For example, as recently pointed out by the General Secretary of the European Trade Union Confederation, there are "unmistakable signs that Europe is engaged in a process of change which promises to effect a profound transformation, a sort of metamorphosis, of our life-style and our model of society" (Gabaglio, 1994, p.7). If the strategic complexities confronting trade unions are generally recognized, more difficult and less apparent are suggested solutions designed to engage with these complexities. At one level, this is understandable. The problems are of a formidable character, strategic in nature and extend beyond the traditional realms of trade unionism; as Gabaglio points out, they are "societal" in nature. On the other hand, the available evidence does suggest a certain caution and hesitancy by trade unions in responding to these changes. As Muckenberger and his colleagues noted:

> There is agreement within the discussion among the trade unions about the need for a fundamental reform with structure and programs of their organization. Despite this agreement, however, trade union practice as such has not undergone any obvious change. The trade unions have taken up a defensive position in an attempt to safeguard their achievements (Muckenberger et al., 1995, p.15).

Despite continuing membership decline, the situation over the last six years has not significantly changed.

This chapter will focus on the contribution of British trade unions to the development of workplace learning. The case of trade unions and workplace learning has been seen only recently as an area of importance, and therefore it lacks substantial evidence and evaluative data. However, it does provide an interesting illustration of trade unions in a particular country attempting, through their educational and training activities, to explore more inclusive activities that begin to address a more "modernized" agenda. If Fred Block is correct in suggesting that the "master concept" – that of industrial society – is no longer "persuasive" for "making sense of our own society" (Block, 1990, p.11), then the example of workplace learning provides an illuminating example of British trade unions attempting to come to grips, in one particular area at least, with what Block calls the "post-industrial" society. Or, to put it another way, the example of workplace learning can be seen as an attempt by some British unions to distance themselves from the concerns and limitations of Fordism and to begin exploring the implications implicit within a post-Fordist perspective.

This is not necessarily the articulated position nor the language that is used by trade unions themselves to discuss or legitimate the development and promotion of workplace learning. Indeed, there is a general absence within the trade union literature of any attempt to conceptually clarify or theoretically relate these developments to wider forces of societal change. As a consequence, it could be argued there is an apparent pragmatic adjustment by trade unions to the development of workplace learning. While this might be the case in many instances and within many unions, there are sufficient hints and suggestions available to tentatively indicate that workplace learning is part of a wider reforming agenda being pursued by the trade unions.

The first part of this chapter will outline the policy context that has encouraged the development of recent workplace learning initiatives in Britain. It will be suggested that a particular combination of initiatives of a political and socio-economic nature have encouraged the involvement of trade unions in the development of workplace learning. In the second part to this chapter, a selection of workplace learning initiatives will be discussed. A number of distinct but interrelated themes will be identified that situate workplace learning within a wider agenda of trade union reform. The final section to the chapter will conclude with several evaluative points that help situate the significance of workplace learning for trade unions, now and in the years ahead.

Before outlining the policy context, brief mention should be made of conceptual ambiguities surrounding understandings of workplace learning. The term "workplace learning" is of recent origin in its popular usage and reflects, in the move away from vocational education and training (VET) of the 1980s and early 1990s, the absorption and largely uncritical acceptance of equating knowledge and skill acquisition with economic competitiveness, productivity and survival. Suddenly, after a century of neglect, a "learning workforce" or a "learning company" or a "learning society" has assumed central significance in policy development (at least at a *rhetorical* level) in Britain and elsewhere. The essentially contested nature of workplace learning renders an accepted definition unlikely or, at least, debatable. Payne and Thomson, for example, draw a distinction between workplace education and training (focusing on skills for immediate work requirements and transferable skills for future job roles) and that of trade union education and training (with its focus on workplace union representative training and working life education) (Payne & Thomson, 1998). Others such as the 1998 *Workplace Learning for the Twenty-first Century Report* see workplace learning as "that learning which derives its purpose from the context of employment. It should address the needs and interests of a variety of stakeholders including employees, potential employees, employers and government" (Sutherland, 1998, p.3). In addition to the ambiguities surrounding the nature of workplace learning, the very socio-economic changes that provide workplace learning with its significance increasingly erode the distinction between "trade union" as opposed to "workplace" education, training and learning. This chapter will focus primarily on trade union education, training and learning activities that focus upon, and derive their significance from, the workplace as a site of learning.

The shift towards workplace learning

The increasing significance of workplace learning over the last two decades can be situated within several different, and sometimes contested, perspectives. Tomassini, for example, mentions the creation of a new paradigm of training where "attention is beginning to shift from the regularity of work performances (organized within well-defined jobs and stable qualifications) to their usefulness in connection with quality and competitiveness" (Tomassini, 2000). Knowledge transformation, he suggests, is now a more complex and integral function of the work situation requiring a greater appreciation and recognition of tacit knowledge that corresponds to "know-why," "know-how," and "know-who." The emphasis today is not only on the transfer of knowledge (the traditional perspective) but more importantly, on facilitating knowledge-conversion (the "new paradigm").

This move towards the centrality of knowledge, of course, is seen as a key component of the new workplace. Within the long-term occupational shifts towards non-manual employment, restructured work patterns and relationships are seen as replacing old-style command and control management and encouraging instead co-ordination based on managing ideas. Thompson and Warhurst (1998), however, after reviewing the evidence and despite acknowledging that powerful forces *have* been reshaping the world of work, conclude that "Despite the bewildering number of change programmes and grade new titles for people and practices, the 'new workplace' is still easily recognisable for the vast majority who too often remain poorly motivated, overworked and undervalued" (Thompson & Warhurst, 1998, p.19).

"Motivation", "empowerment" and "adaptability" within a framework of "flexibility" is the new language of Human Resource Management (HRM) and is usually seen as legitimating the privileged place of knowledge within the "new workplaces". Committed workers are seen as more productive workers. As the advocates of human capital put it, "the quality of human effort can be greatly improved and its productivity enhanced through investing in human capital" (Schultz, 1977, p.313). Winning employees' commitment through diverse strategies is the new goal of management thinking. To slightly re-phrase this point, the issue of "employee subjectivity" has emerged as a key area of new management practices, and workplace learning is often seen as an essential part in the capture of this subjectivity for achieving corporate objectives. To some extent, ironically, it was this emergence of the HRM perspective in the 1980s and 1990s that provided the legitimacy and the political space for trade union workplace learning initiatives that previously had been ideologically closed or blocked.

At the centre of new forms of wealth creation is the ability of workplace and corporate strategies to exploit the skills, knowledge and insights of employees. This intention has a resonance beyond the workplace and HRM. It forms a centrepiece of a post-Fordist discourse seen to increasingly inform government policy in, at least, advanced capitalist societies and probably elsewhere as well (OECD, 1997). The growing interest in "knowledgeability in work," as Thompson and Warhurst (1998, p.7) put it (rather than the more optimistic and uncritical notion of knowledge workers), has been assisted not only by the changes and *continuity* of traditional Taylorist and Fordist strategies but also by the emergence of lifelong learning as a dominant policy framework. Lifelong learning, it seems, is everywhere the framework within which workplace learning in particular, and adult learning more generally, is to be situated. Despite the growing recognition that the term risks losing its purchase and analytical edge, it is lifelong learning that is seen as supporting the strategic vision, legitimacy and policy drive underpinning workplace learning in Britain and elsewhere.

For several reasons, then, and in a number of different ways, the issue of workplace learning has emerged as an increasingly important agenda issue within industrial relations and within economic and educational circles. Trade unions in Britain, as the sections below will illustrate, have reacted positively, although not uncritically, to this shift. As the General Secretary of Britain's largest general union remarked when talking of HRM (quoted in Martinez & Weston, 1992, p.215):

> a new era of crafty Rambo managers has come into existence which seeks to ignore and deliberately disrupt union organization and collective bargaining procedures, by bringing in their own schemes based on fake committees and centred on the individual worker, not the organized worker, with the aim of undermining established working practices and bargaining methods. (Transport & General Workers Union, 1989, p.4)

In the last decade, any trade union members and employees have had to steer a delicate and often frustrating course between the initiatives of "crafty Rambo managers" and those who genuinely advance learning opportunities.

British trade unions and workplace learning

After the wintry conditions of the Conservative Government (1979-1997), British trade unions in the 1990s were seeking collective bargaining opportunities and new strategic justifications for rebuilding their workplace presence and political weight at a national policy level. The launch by the Trades Union Congress (TUC) in the early 1990s of the national Bargaining for Skills initiative provided one such opportunity of unions seeking to exist within the continuing hostile political environment of a Conservative Government. More importantly, it represented a strategic illustration of "new unionism," of trade unions repositioning and reformulating their role and contribution to the changed circumstances confronting them in the mid-1990s. As the TUC stated at its re-launch in 1994, this entailed "shaking off outdated practices and transforming the TUC into a modern, progressive organization which campaigns on behalf of trade unions and working people" (TUC, 1994, p.9). While maintaining a critical distance, the new modernizing approach increasingly stressed the importance of partnership with employers and with training and educational agencies at local and, where possible, national level. Policy statements such as the (1997) *Partners for Progress: Next Steps for the New Unionism* and in 1999, *Partners for Progress: New Unionism at the Workplace* stressed the increasing importance of industrial partnerships for trade unions. Throughout the 1990s and especially in the post-1997 Labour Government period the increasingly warm embrace of partnerships by trade unions signalled and promoted the new role. As the General Secretary of the TUC, John Monks, put it, "The agenda is to improve both organizational performance and the quality of working life for union members. Collective bargaining, yes – but matched by a commitment to joint problem-solving across an agenda of training, skills and career development" (quoted in Brown, 2000, p.305). As Brown illustrates, the endorsement of partnerships by the TUC and affiliated unions was part of a broader strategy designed to regain the initiative in building relationships with employers. An Organising Academy was established, and a 10-year program was launched to substantially restructure and reduce the number of unions and promote single unions covering single industries.

From an educational perspective, the new thinking was being promoted through the Learning Service Task Group, established by the TUC and involving most of the unions. Established in 1997, the Task Group was asked to consider:

> key areas in which the TUC and unions could add value to the opportunities available to members and to develop practical proposals . . . designed to provide a high profile role for the TUC and trade unions as providers and/or facilitators of vocational and other learning opportunities for members and potential members (TUC, 1998, p.13).

As the TUC saw it, a "new framework for workplace learning" is legitimated and related to "the new Lifelong Learning culture" and to the emergence of "a real political will to create a learning society." Although the ideas underpinning such an analysis remain critically undeveloped, there is a strong thematic concern with "the learning divide" historically characterizing participation rates in workplace learning opportunities. Widening provision, guidance, childcare facilities and financial support towards any tuition fees and study costs were suggested as contributions towards addressing this learning divide. The "shared commitments" – between the employer, the State, the trade union and the employee learner – is, argued the TUC, about workplace learning initiatives that enhance employability as well as "developing active citizens with the skills to learn and to participate in a democratic society with their workplace and local communities" (ibid, p.3).

It is perhaps this emphasis on "grass roots members" that provides one of the new emphases by trade unions in recent workplace learning developments. Instead of targeting only their lay-representatives within the workplace, the members (and importantly, potential members) are the new targeted constituencies. As the Communication Workers Union (CWU) states:

> The CWU is using different routes to enable its members to access union education services. For people who are comfortable with the technology, we are using Internet as the main management and delivery system to provide learning and training, in partnership with employers (Ward, 2000, p.5).

The partnerships range from Basic Skills and Information Computer Technology courses through to higher education degree-level courses, and the CWU sees these learning partnerships with employers as "working together to deliver a better trained, more skilful workforce equipped to exploit the opportunities in the ever changing global communications industry" (ibid.). The emphasis on provision of membership opportunities through on-line accredited learning has similarly been developed between the Manufacturing, Science & Finance (MSF) Union and the University of Leeds, while Basic Skills courses for members are being promoted by a variety of trade unions such as the shop workers, engineers and Transport & General Workers (TGWU).

Underpinning such workplace learning schemes is often the notion of "employee development." Although obviously of an ideological and highly contestable nature, the term is usually used within a non-polemical context and is seen as justifying and legitimizing those workplace-learning developments which are broader than task or job-specific training. Indeed, there has arisen a largely unexamined and uncritical language of "ad hoc-ery" which differentiates between workplace educational, training and learning initiatives that prioritize a task and job-specific focus and those which are of a career or employee development nature. It is the latter that are usually placed towards the workplace-learning end of the spectrum and are often, although not always, situated within joint consultative procedures within the workplace rather than the more formal collective bargaining procedures. Employee development schemes in Britain have a comparatively recent tradition and traditionally are seen to have arisen from the well-publicized scheme at Ford Motor Car Company (UK) at the end of the 1980s (Beattie, 1997; Forrester et al., 1995). These schemes, seen as an important part of workplace learning by the Labour Government, are defined by the TUC as:

> programmes supported by employers and unions which are jointly managed by employees to provide the whole workforce with opportunities for personal development . . . and cover a wide range of personal, academic and leisure interests ranging from a hobby or sport to the chance to improve basic skills and to gain academic qualifications including degrees (TUC, 1996, p.53).

Closely aligned to the notion of employee development has been the more recent emphasis on workplace "learning centres." Intended to offer facilities, such as ICT, learning advisors, tutors and guidance, the centres are designed to increase and widen the participation of employees – and in some cases, employees' families and/or local unemployed people – in various learning schemes. Examples of such learning centres include the "cyber café" at the Ford Dagenham plant, the ICT-based centre at the Premier Brands plant, the Lambeth Healthcare Trust and Vauxhall's Luton plant. In Manchester, trade unionists from the bank and retail trade unions are jointly involved in the City Centre Learning Centre. The project worker from the learning centre reports:

> In the retail sector, there is no tradition of work-related training or learning as part of a lifelong agenda. Most workers in that sector do not see learning as relevant to them. We are trying to change that culture and get them to recognise that they can and should learn (TUC, 1999, p.16).

Perhaps the most significant development for workplace learning initiatives, however, has been the promotion of workplace "learning representatives." As suggested in the TUC Learning Services Report,

> trade unions could help ignite a learning revolution in this country . . . . Such positive union involvement is very much dependent on union representatives having the understanding and the skills to help and deliver lifelong learning at the workplace . . . we need to create a union learning representative [who] will be the key player (TUC, 1998, p.3-5).

Whether labelled as union learning representatives, learning advisors or learning advocates, the role and function of advising and promoting learning opportunities to workplace members and employees has been developed by most British trade unions (York Consulting, 2000). Early research studies (Ross, 2000; Payne, 2000) indicate the complexities inherent in such a responsibility. As Ross reports of the experience within one particular union,

Outcomes have been uneven, agendas have been narrowly determined and Learning Representatives have sought to deliver projects in frequently hostile conditions. Whether it is lack of time or the resistance of employers, it has not been easy for Learning Representatives (Ross, 2000, p.75).

Despite these and other problems, it seems clear that the promotion of Learning Representatives represents a significant and important new development by British trade unions.

If employee development schemes, workplace learning centres and the promotion of learning representatives represent some of the recent preoccupations of trade unions when seeking to advance the workplace learning opportunities of their members, then some of the organizational reforms within the unions themselves can be seen as designed to support and encourage these workplace developments. UNISON, for example, is the largest British union and has restructured its union educational provision into its *Open College*. Providing a learning framework structured around four levels, the Open College situates and provides accredited learning pathways for UNISON members ranging from short induction courses and shop-steward training through to vocational professional courses and university degree courses. Some 150 educational "partnership agreements" have been concluded with major employers (mainly in the local authority and health sectors). As the Director of Education in UNISON reported,

> A major benefit is the creation of opportunities for members to progress through other forms of adult and continuing education and to enhance their career prospects. It also helps individuals to increase their skills and confidence enabling them to play a greater role in their own communities, UNISON, and the wider labour movement (quoted in Payne & Thomson, 1998, p.25).

Similarly, the Iron and Steel Trades Confederation has established *Steel Partnership Training* involving the Union and various partners – such as local authorities and universities – to widen the learning opportunities traditionally available for members, employees and those living in steel communities and regions of the country. A third example of organizational reform within unions which supports the new framework of learning is *Learning through Life*, the lifelong learning organization for civil, public and allied service employees which was officially launched in late 1998. Supported by the three main civil service trade unions and the employers, *Learning through Life* aimed to provide a one-stop shop for learning which provided information, advice and guidance in the first instance and then a range of "learning products" from on-line distance learning through to various more traditional courses of a trade union, as well as professional development, character.

The examples listed above suggest the beginnings of significant changes in the organization and provision of trade union education amongst British trade unions.

Everyone benefits

The TUC, and British unions in general, are clear on the rationale under-pinning the development of workplace learning. As the General Secretary of the TUC remarked,

> Learning isn't icing on the cake or an optional extra for trade unions. It's our business. It underpins our members well-being and future prosperity . ... [We have] to make trade union membership count for new generations of workers for whom the steady job is history (Monks, 1999, p.2).

In terms of the "modernizing" agenda that some see as a necessary part of trade union reform and restructuring – as indicated in the introduction to this chapter – it could be argued that the development of workplace learn-ing initiatives represents the best illustrations to date of British trade unions attempting to engage with this "metamorphosis of our life-style and our model of society."

However, a certain caution and even unease in the progress of trade unions and workplace learning is detectable. It is the industrial relations implications of workplace learning that has led to most comment. In some instances, for example, workplace-learning representatives have been nominated, either by the employers or in consultation with the employees before the national trade union has clarified the constitutional position of these lay-representatives. In isolated but important cases, this has resulted in the trade unions (or at least the significant trade union within the sector) refusing to recognize or support workplace-learning representatives (or even use of the term). More significant, though, have been the suspicions of some trade unions of the employers' enthusiasm for partnerships. Although no British trade union has rejected a partnership perspective (with some enthusiastically endorsing them), there remains an element of caution, especially in those instances where the propos-als and initiative for a partnership were instigated by the employers. Some commentators have seen the development of partnerships as indicative of a shift in union governance towards more centralized structures (and control) and away from local activism and as a shift towards individual services rather than a collectivist approach (Heery & Kelly, 1994). Others, such as Brown (2000, p.307), see the move to more co-operative relationships with employers as "in part a symptom of a weakened union movement." However, in an examination of workplace learning partnerships between UNISON and vari-ous employers, Munro and Rainbird refute the automatic association of educational partnerships with that of a more co-operative form of trade union-ism. Instead, their central argument "is that the expansion of individual services can support rather than contradict a participative relationship between union and member" and conclude that "partnerships and services can reaffirm the function and character of unions as agents of collective pur-pose" (Munro & Rainbird, 2000, p.237).

Conclusion

Union-Employer partnerships will obviously be a major focus of inquiry and debate in the years ahead. As far as those concerned with workplace learning, there is little dispute about the undeniable pedagogic benefits resulting from these developments for the participants or their significant contribution towards involving previously excluded or marginalized groups of employees. Instead, the hesitancy arises from the place and purpose of this learning within the wider, supposedly new paradigm of knowledge transformation and cohesion in the "new workplaces." Given the centrality of employees skills, knowledge and experiences for management strategies in the brave new world of post-Fordism, it is understandable that a certain caution characterizes trade union approaches to joint workplace learning initiatives.

REFERENCES

- Beattie, A. (1997). *Working people & lifelong learning: A study of the impact of an employee development scheme.* Leicester: NIACE.

- Block, F. (1990). *Post-industrial possibilities: A critique of economic discourse.* Berkeley: University of California Press.

- Brown, W. (2000). Putting partnership into practice in Britain: Annual review article. *British Journal of Industrial Relations,* 38(2), 299-316.

- Forrester, K., Payne, J. & Ward, K. (1995). *Workplace learning perspectives on education, training and work.* Aldershot: Avebury.

- Gabaglio, E. (1994). The ETUC & trade union education. *Agenda 94 European Trade Union Education.* ETUC: Brussels.

- Heery, E. & Kelly, J. (1994). Professional, participative & managerial unionism: An interpretation of change in trade unions. *Work, Employment and Society,* 8 (1), 11-22.

- Martinez L., & Weston, S. (1992). Human resource management & trade union responses: Bringing the politics of the workplace into the debate. In P. Blyton & P. Turnbull (Eds.), *Reassessing human resource management* (pp. 215-232). London: Sage Publications.

- Monks, J. (1999). Introduction. In *Learning with the unions: A showcase of successful projects sponsored by the Union Learning Fund.* London: Congress House.

- Muckenberger, U., Stroh, C. & Zoll, R. (1995). The challenge of modernization: Towards a new paradigm for trade unions in Europe? *Transfer* 1 (1), 14-30.

- Munro, A. & Rainbird, H. (2000). The new unionism & the new bargaining agenda: UNISON-employer partnerships on workplace learning in Britain. *British Journal of Industrial Relations,* 38(2), 223-240.

- OECD. (1997). *Employment outlook,* Paris: OECD.

- Payne, J. & Thomson, A. (1998). *Partnerships for learning: Opportunities for trade unions and the University for Industry.* Leicester: NIACE.

- Ross, C. (2000). *What works? MSF, lifelong learning & the workplace learning representative.* London: Manufacturing, Science & Finance Union.

- Schultz, T. (1977). Investment in human capital. In J. Kareobel & A.H. Halsey (Eds.), *Power & ideology in education* (pp. 313-324). Oxford: OUP.

- Sutherland, J. (1998). *Workplace learning for the twenty-first century: Report of the Workplace Learning Task Group*, no place.

- Thompson, P. & Warhurst, C. (1998). Hands, hearts & minds: Changing work & workers at the end of the century. In Thompson & Wards (eds.), *Workplaces of the future* (pp. 1-24). London: Macmillan.

- Tomassini, M. (2000). Knowledge dynamics, communities of practice: Emerging perspectives on training. *European Vocational Training Journal,* 19, 38-47.

- Trades Union Congress. (1994). *Partners for progress: Next steps for the new unionism,* London: Congress House.

- Trades Union Congress. (1996). *Partners for lifelong learning.* London: Congress House.

- Trades Union Congress. (1998). *Learning with the unions: A showcase of successful projects sponsored by the Union Learning Fund.* London: Congress House.

- Ward, D. (2000). New ways to study. In *Unions today,* London: Congress House.

- York Consulting. (2000). *Union learning representatives survey report 1.* London: Congress House.

14
Union E-Learning in Canada

JEFFERY TAYLOR

The labour movement has always made some use of distance learning and related technologies in its educational activity. In countries such as Canada and Australia, in particular, with relatively sparse populations spread across vast distances, it has been necessary to use distance education to reach union activists. This has always been a minority current, however, and has most often existed as an add-on to the more substantial face-to-face programs. Since 1995, however, with the development of the World Wide Web and the expansion of interest in and use of the Internet, distance learning has become trendy. Many unions have integrated computer communications into their operations through the use of e-mail and the development of Web sites. And some are beginning to investigate how these new technologies may be used to enhance learning opportunities for their members. In some cases, unions are willing to experiment with computer-based learning (e-learning); in others, a traditional labour skepticism towards technological change means that the new approaches are rejected. This chapter uses Canada as a case study to highlight a recent union-based e-learning initiative and to place the labour movement's use of distance learning and educational technologies in historical perspective.

Distance learning and educational technology before computers

In order to improve and enhance their teaching across a large country, Canadian labour educators have made extensive and, at times, innovative use of educational technologies and distance learning. Conventional distance education has been a feature of Canadian labour education at least since the Canadian Brotherhood of Railway Employees developed steward training and other courses in the 1940s to serve a membership spread along thousands of miles of rail lines. The Labour College of Canada, which has provided advanced (university level) union education since 1963, added a distance education component to its offerings in 1965. While some enrolled in the distance education course in order to prepare for the residential session, as was its original purpose, many took it as a stand-alone activity because they were unable to attend the residential program for the required one to two months (its length has varied over the years). Joe Morris, Canadian Labour Congress (CLC) president in the 1970s, maintained that "one of the best things we ever did was set up the correspondence course program" because it enabled rank-and-file activists, who he claimed criticized the leadership and kept alive the movement's democratic principles, to have access to advanced education. For the first 30 years of its existence, the program was administered solely by the college. Beginning in 1996, however, the college entered into a collaboration with Athabasca University, Canada's open and distance learning university, to offer a three-credit labour studies course as the college's distance education program. This new arrangement allowed the college to move from an older "correspondence" model, in which students worked completely on their own with print materials, to a contemporary distance education approach incorporating student-tutor interaction through telephone and computer communications.

Canadian labour's experience with educational technology, meanwhile, dates from the 1930s. Over the years, labour educators have used radio, filmstrips, film, television, video and other techniques to enhance their offerings and reach members. In the 1930s, for example, the Workers' Educational Association (WEA) began using filmstrips in the face-to-face teaching that it was doing. A filmstrip was a roll of 35 millimetre film on which was printed a number of still pictures and text. Strips were developed on various labour themes and shown at meetings or in educationals in order to stimulate discussion. Thirty years later a group of union education departments experimented with programmed instruction, a highly structured educational technique. Programmed instruction (PI) courses consisted of a number of booklets, with each containing about 70 questions laid out in a planned sequence with each question building on the information that preceded it. PI's promoters claimed that the technique was designed to actively involve the student in the learning process, to provide the student with meaningful immediate feedback, and to be tested and revised until it taught at a predictable level. It was different than a standard instructional manual, its developers argued, in that a PI booklet interacted and communicated with the student while a manual simply presented facts. Detractors, who apparently were a minority among Canadian labour educators at the time, believed that the technique resulted in mechanical learning, while those in unions who used the system viewed it as just another teaching aid to be used either in the classroom or for distance teaching. The Canadian Union of Public Employees (CUPE), the United Steelworkers of America and some other unions bought substantial numbers of PI courses in the late 1960s and used them for several years thereafter in classroom and distance teaching.

During the 1970s and 1980s, meanwhile, the CLC developed a significant audio-visual department at its Labour Education and Studies Centre. A substantial portion of the centre's budget (perhaps one-third or more annually) was devoted to the production and reproduction of audiotapes, videotapes, slides and transparencies. Some of the department's capacity was used to create multi-media components for the course materials that the centre was developing. For example, slides were produced to accompany the CLC's basic stewards course and the centre's health and safety course, while videos were shot for its two organizing courses. But a large part of the department's time was consumed by special projects and requests from affiliates. Two years after it was formed, the audio-visual coordinator was complaining that the department was overburdened, and that 70 percent of its time was spent responding to outside requests while 30 percent was spent on centre business. The output ranged from the simple recording of speeches and other activities at conferences or meetings, which seemed to consume most of the department's time, to more highly produced features dealing with specific issues or campaigns. One of the first video projects was a series of interviews with labour leaders and retired staffers talking about their experiences in the labour movement. In another project, in which video was used to support an organizing drive, fishers in the Maritime provinces were featured discussing their problems and why they were supporting the Maritime Fishermen's Union.

The most successful labour use of educational technology in Canada prior to the development of computer communications, however, was organized by the WEA during the 1940s. The association was able to take advantage of publicly owned communications resources that were available during the Second World War to institute labour-related radio programming and a Trade Union Film Circuit that included some union-specific film production. The WEA-produced *Labour Forum* was heard on the national network of the Canadian Broadcasting Corporation (CBC) during 1942 and 1943, and was managed by a committee composed of the WEA, the CBC and the two national labour centrals in the country. *Labour Forum* programs featured actual workers reading WEA-prepared scripts that explored various problems and issues, including profit gouging, poor planning and ineffective management. Print materials were produced by the association and distributed to listening groups across the country. The series was received enthusiastically by working-class audiences, but business groups complained about the anti-capitalist sentiment that was present in many of the programs. As a result, the government curbed *Labour Forum*'s autonomy during 1943 and eventually had the series cancelled.

Wartime experience with film was slightly more successful as the WEA was able to initiate and manage a labour film program that included the National Film Board and the two national labour centrals. Between 1942 and 1946 a Trade Union Film Circuit operated across the country, bringing labour-related films to trade unionists. Educator-projectionists were hired and trained by the WEA to show the films and ensure that as much as possible they were integrated into educational activities. And discussion trailers, in which actual trade unionists were featured debating the issues raised in the film, were produced for several the films in order to stimulate discussion at the meetings or educational events at which the film was shown. At its peak in 1945 there were 450 showings a month across the country, reaching 40,000 trade unionists. Though the radio and film projects were short-lived and there were limited resources available, the WEA was able to incorporate these new media into a broader workers' education strategy that included film strips, short training institutes, discussion groups, study circles, and university-level instruction (Taylor, 2001).

Solinet

Perhaps because of its long history of experimentation with educational technologies and distance learning, Canada was the site of a pioneering use of union-based computer communications in the 1980s and 1990s. CUPE was the first union in the world to use computer communications in a significant way, and it was arguably the first national organization of any kind in Canada to establish its own computer-communications system. In 1987 Marc Belanger, the unions's technology coordinator, loaded the text-based CoSy e-mail and conferencing system onto a computer at CUPE headquarters in Ottawa and connected the computer to the country's datapac system, which allowed individuals in cities across the country to dial in to a local telephone number using their modem and connect to his computer in Ottawa. In the months and years that followed, a small but significant group of Canadian trade unionists began using Solinet to exchange e-mail among themselves and establish "conferences," or online workshops and meetings. CUPE used Solinet's conferences to facilitate bargaining and carry on subject-specific discussions, but the most interesting parts of Solinet were the conferences that were open to everyone in the Solinet community.

Belanger's philosophy from the beginning was that Solinet should be a service for the whole labour community (first in Canada and later, when the technology permitted, for the whole world). One of the liveliest spaces on the network was the "lounge," where any and all labour-related subjects were discussed. In addition, general subject-specific discussions on topics such as technological change and labour and the New Democratic Party were held periodically. In 1992 Solinet joined forces with the labour studies program at Athabasca University to organize and facilitate a month-long workshop on the general subject of labour education. Later, the Athabasca program used Solinet to conduct its first online offering of a for-credit labour studies course.

As innovative and exciting as Solinet was, its impact and reach were limited to a small number of enthusiasts as long as online communication remained the purview of university researchers and those with a particular interest in new technologies. Things changed with the advent of the World Wide Web in 1995 – which allowed for the use of graphical images, photographs, and eventually sound and video in online communication – and the explosion of interest in the internet. Belanger and Solinet made the leap to the Web with a new conferencing system called Virtual- U that, like the older CoSy-based system, allowed participants to conduct online workshops and meetings but, since it was on the World Wide Web, was accessible to anyone in the world with a Web browser and an Internet account.

In 1996 and 1997 the "new" (Web-based) Solinet and the Athabasca labour studies program collaborated to offer a series of non-credit online labour education workshops. Beginning with a general course called Labour Education and the Internet, designed in part to give potential online facilitators some familiarity with the new medium, the series consisted of 12 month-long workshops covering a range of topics from The Third World and the Internet to Women Organizing. More than one thousand participants from around the (mainly developed and English-speaking) world registered for at least one of these workshops. With the exception of one women-only course, all of the workshops were open to whoever wanted to participate. Facilitators chosen from around the world for their subject-matter expertise contributed their knowledge and guided the discussions. Those participants who responded to online surveys (about 18% of the total) indicated that they enjoyed the opportunity to interact with fellow trade unionists from a variety of countries.

Belanger saw this series as a prototype for an international online labour college. However, if such an enterprise were to develop, it would not be on the network that he had built. The union leadership decided in 1998 that Solinet should only be accessible to CUPE members. A year later Belanger moved on to the International Labour Organization to teach computer communications and, sadly, CUPE disabled Solinet completely. A signficant chapter in the Canadian labour movement's innovative use of new educational technologies was closed (Taylor, 2001; 1996a; 1996b; Spencer & Taylor 1994).

E-Learning and the Canadian Labour Congress

The Athabasca labour studies program, however, continued to operate its own version of Solinet and, at the turn of the century, is working with the CLC to build online educational capacity in the congress. This activity is funded as part of a pan-Canadian Telelearning Network of Centres of Excellence exploring the problems and possibilities of what was called "telelearning" in the 1990s and, increasingly, "e-learning" in the early years of the new century. While much of the research agenda of the larger network is corporate-driven, the CLC-Athabasca project is investigating how computer-based educational technologies can best be integrated into labour education practice.

Contemporary labour education in Canada is worker-centred and activist-focused. In 1994 the CLC's National Education Advisory Committee produced a consensus on the future development of union education in which it concluded that education should infuse all aspects of the local union, and union educators should coordinate their activities more closely with other parts of the labour movement. Furthermore, education activists were urged to share the labour movement's vision for social change, justice and solidarity with young people, equity groups and progressive organizations beyond the workplace. In future, while steward and collective bargaining courses (the core of the traditional union education program) would still be offered, they and other courses would be taught in a way that placed most priority on mobilizing members to engage in a social movement that encompassed the workplace but extended beyond it. The creation of the CLC's Education and Campaigns department in 1997 was designed to facilitate closer cooperation between union educators and activists engaged in a range of ongoing and specific campaigns, including those organized by the congress' new youth coordinator.

A key principle of this activist education is that workers should teach other workers: the persons best suited to facilitate and lead discussions were workers themselves, and emphasis was placed on training and supporting workers in the objectives and principles of adult and popular education. The 20,000 CUPE members who attended one or more courses in a given year during the 1990s, for example, were likely taught by one of the 250 Occasional Facilitators who were trained in popular-education techniques and normally taught courses in teams of two. Peer educators in the Public Service Alliance of Canada's Alliance Facilitators' Network, meanwhile, were trained to identify learning needs and to develop and deliver union education modules locally across the country; they met regularly either locally, regionally or nationally to exchange ideas, methodology and materials to support one another. And the United Steelworkers of America had a network of 140 trained local members across the country, each equipped to instruct a variety of courses when called upon to do so by the union (CLC, 1997; Gereluk, 2001).

But is computer-based education compatible with this approach to labour education? When the purpose of your program is to empower activists through worker-to-worker interaction, is a technology that intervenes between people a help or a hindrance? The CLC-Athabasca research project asks these questions as it investigates if and how e-learning can be integrated into labour educational programs. By mid-2000 the project had conducted two online workshops. The first was designed to train educators and activists in the art of online facilitation and the second brought together labour council activists from across the country to plan and strategize for May Day 2000. The second workshop was conducted entirely online, while the first consisted of a one-day face-to-face orientation followed by an online component. In both cases participants were online together for six weeks in a Web-based computer conference called the Solinet union hall (actually the Virtual U conferencing software from the earlier Solinet that was customized to make it more labour friendly). The online union hall was supplemented for both workshops by a separate Web site that contained workshop outlines and supporting materials. Participants were not expected to be online at the same time, but were asked to visit the Solinet union hall regularly to post comments or to respond to other contributions. Two co-facilitators kept the discussion moving according to the previously arranged and agreed upon workshop structure. Although there was some flexibility in the structure, the general rule was that one week was allotted to each discussion subject.

The Facilitating Online Conferences workshop began with a daylong face-to-face session at a United Food and Commercial Workers Union computer laboratory in Winnipeg, Manitoba (a geographically central location). During the day, the 12 participants digested, criticized and rewrote a proposed structure for the online component of the workshop, and then learned about and practiced using the conferencing software. Two weeks later the Winnipeg attendees were joined by six others in the Solinet union hall to begin the six weeks of online discussion. In their online activity, the participants learned the fundamentals of online facilitation. For example, they were taken through the techniques of maintaining an active conference, listening to each other online, and mediating conflicts. But participants also thought and talked about the similarities and differences between face-to-face and online facilitation. In comparing the two, they noted for example that face-to-face facilitators could rely to a large degree on visual and verbal cues, but that these were absent online (at least in text-based conferencing). The online facilitator had to be more attuned to textual cues, and had to be attentive to the subtleties and nuances of everyone's (textual) contributions.

In 2000 the CLC endorsed May Day for the first time in its history and committed resources and energy to ensuring that the workers' holiday was marked in some way in various communities across the country. Labour councils in some larger centres had been commemorating the day for some years, but this was the first time that an attempt was made to spark interest and activity across the country. The purpose of the online workshop was to link activists in smaller and larger centres so they could share experiences and ideas about May Day mobilizations and commemorations.

Forty-eight people registered for the May Day workshop, about 40 of these contributed at least one message to the workshop, and a core of a dozen or so participants sustained the discussion over its six-week life. The participants were mostly labour council officials or activists from communities as large as Toronto and as small as Pointe Verte, New Brunswick. The workshop was structured as a series of discussions about various aspects of May Day organizing and was held during March and April. After a week of introductions and practice using the computer-conferencing software, discussion moved on to a brief history of May Day and then to planning for actual May Day events in 2000. A small group of participants reassembled in the online union hall for a week in May for a post-May Day assessment of how events transpired in their respective communities.

The purpose of the online workshop, then, was to use computer-communications technology – specifically the online union hall and a
Web site – to link activists in support of a specific educational and mobilizing
event in their communities. Post-workshop interviews with 12 participants
(one-quarter of those registered and slightly less than one-third of participants)
and an analysis of the conference transcripts suggest that the experience was
most useful for activists in smaller communities and that a combination of
online and offline activity created the best learning situations.

Participants based in smaller communities – ranging from cities of 100,000
to towns of 10,000 population – were most likely to find the workshop useful,
while at least one participant from a larger centre claimed s/he had little to
learn from the experiences of those in smaller labour councils. Cities such as
Edmonton, Winnipeg and Toronto had pre-existing May Day celebrations
that were part of weeks-long or month-long MayWorks cultural festivals, and
the range of activities they undertook and supported dwarfed the often
one-event activities that smaller centres mounted. And, of course, there were
many more chances for face-to-face encounters with fellow activists as part of
these larger festivals. But for the activist in a smaller city in British Columbia,
Saskatchewan or Nova Scotia, the virtual contact provided by the computer
conference was an important source of connection to a larger mobilization.
Inspiration could be drawn from the other experiences, and proposals for
activities could be bounced off of more seasoned sisters and brothers. Furthermore, since the conference took place over a six-week period, it was possible
to take an idea away from the online union hall, test it in practice, and then
report back a week or two later. Indeed, some participants reported that the
workshop was most effective for them when it was integrated with existing
"offline" connections, organizations or groups.

One of the most interesting examples of online/offline cross-fertilization
occurred during the week that focused on the history of May Day. Participants
read and discussed a short capsule history from Haymarket to recent events in
South Korea and elsewhere, and were then asked to do some local research in
an attempt to unearth May Day traditions in their own communities. Some
spoke to movement elders, and others actually went to their local library to do
newspaper research. What emerged from this brief exercise were the beginnings of a locally based archive of the history of May Day in Canada. We
learned, for example, about May Day marches in Sudbury, Ontario during
the 1940s and about sympathy strikes in Peterborough, Ontario and elsewhere
in support of the Winnipeg General Strike of 1919.

Overall, participants felt that the first-hand experience in an online workshop gave them important knowledge of the potential value of
computer-based education and that this could be taken back to their local set-
tings, shared with others, and that a more informed decision could be made as
to if, how, why and when to make use of this educational tool. They found the

May Day content itself useful for both bringing back to offline groups and for their own feelings of solidarity with others. Participants said that the activities of others energized them and helped to counter the isolation that can occur with busy schedules and burnout. They felt, though, that for the labour movement to make use of this technology, it had to be linked with existing face-to-face connections and organizational structures. The technology was not a substitute for other educational or organizing initiatives, then, but a means of enhancing them by providing greater information and by making communication participatory and less uni-directional.[38]

Conclusion

The recent development of union e-learning in Canada is part of a broader history of using available educational technologies to enhance the face-to-face interaction that is the heart of labour education. At its best, such as when the WEA tried to integrate film, radio and other media into a mass education strategy, the technology is used as part of a coherent approach that exploits the strengths of the various methods to create the best possible learning opportunities for participants. Canadian trade unionists are just beginning to explore the possibilities of e-learning in the context of a general approach to union education that emphasizes activism and organizing. What is clear so far is that computer-mediated communication offers some benefits, especially as a means of linking activists in remote locations to ongoing events and discussions that otherwise might not be available to them. Furthermore, online interaction is most successful when linked to parallel offline activity. While further research is required to determine what works best in this area, the next step for labour educators is to decide what part e-learning can play in their long-term strategic programming plans.

REFERENCES

- Canadian Labour Congress. (1997). *Canadian labour education at a glance.* Ottawa: Author.
- Gereluk, W. (2001). *Labour education in Canada today.* Athabasca, AB: Athabasca University.
- Spencer, B. & Taylor, J. (Fall, 1994). Labour education in Canada: A Solinet conference. *Labour/Le Travail 34.* 217-237.
- Taylor, J. (2001). *Union learning: Canadian labour education in the twentieth century.* Toronto: Thompson Educational Publishing.
- Taylor, J. (1996a). The continental classroom: Teaching labour studies on-line. *Labor Studies Journal 21*(1). 19-38.
- Taylor, J. (1996b). The Solidarity Network: Universities, computer-mediated communication, and labor studies in Canada. In T. M. Harrison & T. Stephen (Eds.), *Computer networking and scholarly communication in the twenty-first-century university.* 277-290. Albany: State University of New York Press.

[38] 1 "CLC99" and "May Day 2000" conference transcripts at www.vu.vlei.com/vu/solinet; participant interviews conducted by Peter Sawchuk, Summer/Fall 2000.

UNIT V
REFLECTIONS ON THE FUTURE

Michael Newman suggests that unions need to re-evaluate their central purpose and *modus operandi* in the light of developments over the past 20 years. Drawing from the cozy relationships unions enjoyed with Australian Labour governments in the past, and questioning the gains made for members, he asks whether unions are simply striving to represent members within the new global order or should they seek to become key players in civil society? If they choose the latter, there are implications for labour education: the focus of labour education would shift from representative training – core labour education – towards programs stressing education and action for community development, strategic involvement and social justice.

Bruce Spencer and Naomi Frankel review union learning in the context of the challenges presented by new management techniques, workplace learning and the globalization of production. The chapter draws together the themes raised by the different contributions and blends them with other developments in labour education to provide a commentary on the future of labour learning in the new century.

15

Part of the System or Part of Civil Society: Unions in Australia

MICHAEL NEWMAN

This chapter looks at the gains and losses for trade unions in Australia during an extended period of cooperation with government, and asks the question expressed in the chapter's title. It suggests that unions may need to review the roles they play within both the state and civil society. It outlines three interpretations of civil society and uses them to identify the different kinds of union education we might use in the struggle for industrial and social justice.

Government and unions in accord

For 13 years Australia provided a case study of cooperation between the trade unions and the government. The cooperation was formalized in an agreement whose full title was *The Prices and Income Accord* but which quickly became known simply as the *Accord*. The parties to the Accord were the Australian Labor Party (ALP) and the Australian Council of Trade Unions (ACTU).

The ACTU and the ALP negotiated and signed the Accord in 1982. In 1983 the ALP was elected into government at the federal level and remained in government until 1996. The Accord went through several re-negotiations, and there were periods of tension between the two parties, but this special relationship between government and the peak union body lasted the full 13 years.

The Accord covered not just wage fixation but employment policy, methods of combating inflation, industry development, health care, superannuation, and other matters coming under the rubric of the "social wage." The details of agreement were complex and many, and were revised, sometimes radically, as social, economic and political conditions changed. Rather than examine the content of the Accord, however, I want to look at some of the implications of such an agreement actually being in existence.

Implications of the Accord

Under the Accord the ALP agreed that once in government it would establish a range of advisory committees and councils. From 1983 on, therefore, unions were represented on a whole raft of bodies along with government and employers. Through these "tripartite" mechanisms union officials had access to information, formed close associations with senior ministers and public servants, and contributed directly to the formulation of social, political and economic policy. Gains resulted from the unions' involvement in these bodies, and from other commitments made by the parties to the Accord. Distinctive development policies were formulated for different industries. Lower paid workers without industrial muscle benefited from nationally negotiated wage increases. A national health system was reintroduced. And many more workers were drawn into employer funded superannuation schemes.

It could be said, therefore, that during the period of the Accord the unions were in the ascendancy. For example, much was made in the mass media of the close relationship between the Secretary of the ACTU and the two ALP Prime Ministers who held power during those 13 years. If some of the more rabid letter writers in the newspapers were to be believed, the Secretary of the ACTU was to all intents and purposes a member of the Federal Government Cabinet, and the unions were dictating government policy.

However, other features of those 13 years of the Accord make for a different story. Union membership dropped significantly, from over 50 percent of the workforce to just above 30 percent. Decisions affecting union members were taken at the highest level, and the democratic processes at the workplace were weakened. The government implemented economic rationalist policies, such as floating the Australian dollar and lowering or removing import tariffs, and workers in many industries lost their jobs. The country went into recession in the early 1990s, unemployment rose to 11 percent, and many small enterprises closed. Some unionists felt their leaders had lost sight of their major purpose – that of protecting and improving wages and conditions. They objected to their highest body being part of the system.

The system

The term "the system," like the terms "the establishment" or "the elite" or "the bosses," can be used colloquially without clear definition. But the term is also used in critical social theory, and here it has a more specific meaning. Jurgen Habermas (1987) describes the system as being the processes of exchange that make up the economy, and the political and administrative controls that make up the social structures within which we all live. It is the combination of money and power that dictates much of our lives. In this meaning "the system" is sometimes used synonymously with "the state." But we can see the system extending beyond the state to include transnational corporations, international agreements, multinational consortia, and other facets of power and exchange that extend beyond, or transcend, individual governments and administrations.

Under the Accord in Australia, union officials played a part (along with representatives of employers and representatives of government) in deciding on economic policy, matters of trade, investment in industry, taxation policy and the like. There were still times when the ACTU opposed the government, or particular ministers in government. There was a celebrated moment when the Secretary of the ACTU, acting on his Executive Council's decision, opposed the Federal Treasurer's preferred option for tax reform and effectively sank that option. However, for the most part, throughout the 13 years the union movement in Australia was allied to, involved in, and had perhaps even become an integral part of that larger agglomeration of bodies and people engaging in exchange and wielding power. Along with the corporate sector and the government the unions were a part of the system. Union education during this period was constrained by the Accord.

The demise of the Accord

The Accord came to an end when the ALP was removed from government in the 1996 federal elections and replaced by a coalition made up of the Liberal Party as senior partner and the National Party as the junior partner. Since its election this conservative Coalition Government has been no friend to unions. The spirit of tripartism has been abandoned. Legislative "reforms" have been introduced to reduce the power of the unions. It has been made easier for employers to introduce individual workplace contracts in place of collective agreements. Various union rights have been removed or reduced. And the Industrial Arbitration Commission's power to resolve conflicts has been weakened. Symbolic of this new government's attitude to unions and union members was the rapid closure of the Australian Trade Union Training Authority. This government-funded authority had existed for more than 20 years under previous Labor and conservative governments for the purpose of providing and coordinating training for union officials and union members across the country.

Deprived of their direct influence on government, trade unions in Australia have had to reconsider their position. The ALP went on to the opposition benches in parliament and so, whilst no longer in control of government, nonetheless stays clearly within the system as the alternative government in waiting, playing its part in the passage of legislation, in parliamentary committee work and in the representation of constituents. But there is no straightforward position for the unions to adopt in the current system. The new government has not simply downgraded the role unions play in their deliberations: they have excluded them, and adopted an openly hostile attitude towards them. In 1998 during a protracted industrial dispute on the Australian waterfront, the Minister for Industrial Relations openly took sides with management, and was accused by the union involved of actively working to severely weaken or even destroy the union. Unions in Australia still form part of our society, and are still involved in the system through the Industrial Arbitration Commission, the process of negotiating enterprise agreements and industrial awards, and through their involvement in superannuation funds and other economic, social and political institutions. But their position within the current system is compromised, and we can ask whether they should struggle to remain part of the system or whether they should more clearly seek to become a part of civil society.

Civil society

"Civil society" is a concept offered as a counterbalance to the system. Two major commentators on the concept of civil society are Robert Putnam (1993) and Eva Cox (1995). Putnam sees civil society manifested in local government, local institutions, and local organizations. Whilst local, the components of his concept of civil society often have a structure, and are in some formal or semi-formal way recognized entities. Eva Cox extends Putnam's definition to more clearly include all those community groupings with democratic, egalitarian and voluntary structures. She cites as examples sporting clubs, craft groups, local environment associations, some ethnic and religious groups, playgroups, neighbourhood centres and the like. To these she also adds the family and informal groupings of people in the workplace. Cox's vision of civil society would include an agreement two people might make to call in and check on a third elderly neighbour in their street on a daily basis. Whilst their emphases may vary slightly, both Putnam and Cox are describing those accessible gatherings of people at a local level through which we participate in society and give meaning to our everyday social lives.

A challenge to union educators

In many parts of the world unions have always faced hostile governments. In other parts of the world unions have experienced a gradual loss of favour in the eyes of their countries' administrations. In the Australian case (and perhaps in Britain after 1979 and New Zealand in the 1980s), however, the loss of a place at the government table was abrupt. This particular "case study," then, enables us to identify very clearly a major challenge facing union education and training officers in the new century. The challenge: to help union officials and members distinguish between the roles they can play in the system and the roles they can play in civil society, and to provide the theory and information necessary to help them choose which manifestation of society they should engage with.

To be able to do this, union educators will need the freedom to experiment in program design and delivery. They will need to convince their unions that they should move well beyond the roles of instructor and trainer, and be enabled to facilitate search conferences, debates, seminars, open-ended workshops, brainstorming sessions and research projects. In the best of all possible worlds, the union educator will be supported by a committee of senior and influential officials who understand education not as an exercise in instruction, management and control but as a creative, imaginative endeavour in which problems are posed and examined. The educator and her or his program of educational activities will need to be seen as playing a part in the way the union formulates policy and makes major decisions. In the jargon of today, the union should become "a learning organization," that is, a union which develops and grows and changes and engages in its daily activities through the medium of learning.

If the decision is to engage more completely in civil society, then union education programs will need to start by helping make the unions themselves structurally and philosophically more in harmony with the character of civil society. This will mean refocusing on local democratic practices, on workplace representation, and on workplace activism. In Australia this shift is already taking place in a major union's educational program and in an ACTU-sponsored project aimed at union renewal.

The Australian Manufacturing Workers' Union (AMWU) is a major union in Australia, large by Australian standards, and traditionally recognized as the "lead" union. This reputation comes from the fact that for a good part of the twentieth century the AMWU (or one of its antecedents) was often the first to struggle for and gain new levels of pay and new conditions, which then flowed on to workers in other industries across the country. The union recently signalled its commitment to a particular form of educational policy by appointing Don Sutherland to a senior national educational position. Sutherland has extensive experience as an educator in other unions and in a national union education agency. He is committed to union education which facilitates the organizing rather than the service model, and which politicizes workplace representatives and rank-and-file members to take on activist roles. Sutherland sees the organizing model in its turn being subsumed in the larger concept of the "campaigning model," and argues that all union education should be located within an analysis of the political economy and directed towards the mobilization of working people.

But to engage with civil society unions will need to look outside the union movement as a whole and engage with other bodies, organizations and groupings that make up civil society. If union educators are to help their unions do this they will need to identify different forms or interpretations of civil society, and devise initiatives that take these different forms or interpretations into account.

Civil society constructed on trust

In her series of lecturers entitled A *Truly* Civil Society (1995) Cox advocates a form of civil society constructed on trust. She distinguishes between different kinds of capital – financial capital, physical capital, human capital and social capital. She argues that for each of the first three forms of capital, excessive expenditure will lead to its depletion. However, in the case of social capital, the results of excessive expenditure can be the exact opposite. The more we spend, the more we amass. Social capital is the accumulation of trust as a result of cooperation amongst people, and the more we base our relationships on trust, the more trusting all the parties become and the more trust we create.

Unions have not always played a proactive part in civil society. By their very nature they are drawn towards the system. Their concerns are to do with wages and conditions of their members, that is, with economic considerations. And their adversaries are employers, in the forms of corporations and governments, that is, the wielders of power in both the private and public sectors of our economies. But if the civil society described by Putnam and Cox has any validity, then unions need to consider how they can become more involved in this other manifestation of society. Union educators will need to devise programs to help their officials and members examine how to forge relationships with the myriad organizations and groupings that make up civil society. They will need to examine the concept of social capital, and consider the benefits in helping amass it. They will need to provide community profiles and briefings on community issues. They will need to look at the principles and processes of community development and community action, and examine how they resemble and differ from union organization and industrial action. Such an education program might seem at first sight to be wasteful of the union's educational resources but of course it has a thoroughly pragmatic side to it. If a union cooperates effectively with community groups to help them pursue their particular aims, then it may well receive useful, even decisive, community support when it takes industrial action to pursue its own aims.

There are, however, some problems with this vision of a civil society constructed on trust. One is that it has a romantic or utopian feel to it, and the reality does not always live up to the promise. Not all local, voluntary, egalitarian groupings amass social capital. A local neighbourhood centre can be riven with rivalries, for example. Another problem is that a civil society constructed on trust assumes that those in power are essentially civilized and can be trusted too. Another problem is that this vision of civil society is a suburban, mainstream one. It conjures up images of public meetings in town halls, parents' evenings at the local school, people meeting to play tennis and the like. Perhaps unwittingly, some people espousing the concept are in danger of excluding members of certain minority groups, and people leading various kinds of inner city or rural alternative lifestyles. And yet another, and perhaps the most serious, problem is that by the very act of focusing on social capital, this vision of civil society sidelines itself from the economy where, whether we like it or not, decisions that affect every one of us are taken.

Civil society as a site for struggle

Because of these possible weaknesses in this first, essentially gentle, vision of civil society, it may be useful to look for "harder" versions of civil society, and devise educational responses to those as well. Antonio Gramsci (1971) described civil society as being made up of institutions such as schools and universities, enterprises, and the church. He saw these institutions as "ramparts of the state", shoring it up and reinforcing its hegemonic control. Gramsci distinguished between "a war of maneouvre" and "a war of position." In a war of maneouvre, armies join battle and seek to defeat each other through the strategic deployment of their forces. In a war of position, forces gain entry to the ramparts and fight from within. Activists, Gramsci argued, needed to understand the organizations making up civil society as sites of struggle. They needed to gain entry to these ramparts of the state in order to disrupt, deter, and alter their policies and practices. Since these organizations promulgated the ideas and authority of the state, this kind of action had the potential to bring about significant social and political change.

With this harder concept of civil society in mind, union educators will need to provide programs dealing with infiltration, persuasion, provoking and managing change, subversion even. Such educational programs will need to help union members develop understandings of how organizations work, and how they can be influenced. Union educators will need to collect case studies and recount stories of people engaging in wars of position. One such story is of activists from the women's movement in Australia during the 1980s seeking positions within the bureaucracies of the state, within high-level welfare bodies and within other influential organizations such as the churches, and bringing about changes from within. The work of these "femocrats" resulted in the introduction and refinement of laws relating to equity and discrimination in employment, changes in the welfare system, and shifts in community attitudes to questions of gender (see Eisenstein, 1991).

Civil society as an alternative form of participation

A third form of civil society is to be found in new social movements, those large, sometimes massive, groupings of people united by a common interest in promoting or resisting some form of social, economic or political change. Social movements provide us with alternative ways of participating in the affairs of our communities and societies. People in social movements join together and take part in letter-writing campaigns, consumer boycotts, demonstrations, strikes and the like, and so engage in direct forms of participation in the affairs of society. This kind of participation can have an effect. A number of recent social movements have brought about huge social change. These include the women's movement, environmentalists, the indigenous people's movement, and the vast collection of people combating the spread of the HIV/AIDS virus and caring for sufferers.

To help unions engage in this kind of civil society, union educators will need to help officials and members learn about the theory, histories and categories of social movements. They will need to distinguish between structured social movements like the churches, semi-structured social movements like the environmentalists, and unstructured social movements like those people responding to the HIV/AIDS virus. They will need to examine the phases social movements move through, from initial agitation to consolidation to institutionalization to bureaucratization to either eradication or transformation. They will need to research examples of different kinds of cross-movement cooperation, and examine ways of forming effective relationships in the forms of complicities, alliances or solidarities with movements with similar ideals (Newman, 1999).

Conclusion

In the Australian "case study" there are examples of different kinds of cross-movement cooperation. A wide variety of political parties, action groups and community organizations gave their support at marches and pickets during the recent Australian Maritime Union's waterfront dispute. Unions joined with political parties, social justice action groups and churches on the same platforms and in joint demonstrations to put pressure on the Australian Government to intervene in the recent crisis in East Timor. And recent "corporate campaigning" has brought consumer groups into alliance with unions to protest the closure of local branches of various banks and the consequent downsizing of those banks' workforce.

There are examples of unions and unionists entering the ramparts of the state and unions have involved themselves in community activities and community events, for example through APHEDA, the union-sponsored international aid agency, or through the Trade Union Choir, which performs at conferences, festivals and community events. Despite these examples, it is my belief that there has been little organized reflection on the experience these examples have provided, and that little organized learning has grown out of them.

The abrupt loss of a place at the government table following the 1996 federal election makes it necessary for Australian unions to rethink their position in society, to devise new political and industrial strategies, and to forge new kinds of relationship with other sectors of society. Union educators can draw on all three ideas of civil society in the design and implementation of programs to help the union movement achieve this. The intention of these programs would be to develop a form of unionism that can generate social capital at a local community level, can engage in strategic action within the structure of the state, and can forge alliances with other social movements committed to the struggle for social justice.

REFERENCES

* Cox, E. (1995). *A truly civil society: 1995 Boyer lectures.* Sydney: ABC Books.

* Eisenstein, H. (1991). *Gender shock: Practicing feminism on two continents.* Boston: Beacon Press.

* Gramsci, A. (1971). (eds. Hoare, Q. & Smith, G.N.) *Selections from the Prison Notebooks of Antonio Gramsci.* New York: International Publishers.

* Habermas, J. (1987). *The theory of communicative action,* Vol 2. Cambridge: Polity Press.

* Newman, M. (1999). *Maeler's regard: Images of adult learning.* Sydney: Stewart Victor Publishing.

* Putnam, R. (1993). *Making democracy work: Civic tradition in modern Italy.* New Jersey: Princeton University Press.

16
Unions and Learning in a Global Economy

BRUCE SPENCER AND NAOMI FRANKEL

A nyone who has studied union organization and behaviour recognizes that, at best, unions are contradictory social formations. They represent workers' opposition to employer and state authority and at the same time negotiate the terms of workers' compliance to that authority. In many cases they have become reliant on state legislation in order to function, with disastrous results when that legislation was reversed as was experienced for example in New Zealand, the UK and Australia in the 1980s and 1990s. In Scandinavian countries unions remain popular organizations with very high membership densities, but many would argue they have lost their ability to act independently within the comfortable embrace of social partnership. In South Africa they emerged from the struggle against apartheid as revolutionary organizations but have since been struggling to find a new role as bargaining agents and as advocates for the least advantaged workers. But no matter how you view the essence of unionism, they are important organizations of working people, and they do represent the potential for democratic challenge at work and in society. Even if this challenge is to be understood as a relatively weak countervailing power to that of capital, a power that can only moderately influence terms and conditions, it is still important for workers. Obviously what is happening to unions influences labour education; labour education inevitably reflects the broader position of labour in society. Labour educators both inside and outside the unions push and pull on the limits of possibility, arguing for differing positions based on their own analysis of how far the union movement can go in mounting a democratic challenge at work and in society.

Unions and the learning rhetoric

The current rhetoric around "workplace learning," "teamwork," and "the learning organization" in the context of what are referred to as the "knowledge economy" and the "learning society" has had an impact on labour education. These new descriptors of corporate and state activity in the context of globalization of production are often cited to marginalize the significance of unions and therefore the irrelevance of labour education. We need to remember that workplace learning, as defined by employers, is essentially about learning to become a more efficient and compliant "human resource." While the enthusiasm for teamwork may have some advantages for some workers, it has to be understood within the context of human capital theory and new human resource management strategies that seek to bypass the kind of workplace democracy that independent unionism can provide. In some cases teamwork has also gone hand in hand with downsizing. This new rhetoric emphasizes unitary perspectives of workplace activity and workplace culture. Workers are described as "stakeholders," they are all asked to "share the vision;" gone is the grudging acceptance of pluralism, of the recognition that from time to time workers do have legitimate differences with employers which can be settled through the quasi-democratic procedures of negotiation and agreement. Today the independent voice of labour is to be silenced while the sole authority of the employer is masked by the description of workers as "partners," "members" or "associates." In the UK freely negotiated recognition agreements are being displaced by "partnership agreements" that emphasize employer rights including denying the rights of workgroups to democratically determine their own union steward! (Wray, 2001). Never was it more important for unions to establish their legitimacy and their own, distinctive education programs.

Labour education

This book has been able to review aspects of labour education as it is being practiced in several countries spanning all continents. Labour education is an important ongoing union activity that is often ignored academically. This is partly because, in many instances, unions undertake this education work themselves, beyond the gaze of the academy, and partly because unions are wary of academics, reluctant to encourage academic enquiry into their activity. We have provided illustrations of some of the ways in which labour education is broadening out from core training of workplace representatives to addressing some of the newer issues posed by workplace learning, globalization and the learning society.

New developments in core labour education

This collection has not focused on the majority provision of continuing core labour education of local representatives, typically termed "shop steward" training. This important work is ever changing, with perhaps more emphasis on peer tutoring in one country and significant content changes in another (for a recent survey and discussion of Canadian provision see Gereluk, 2001; for European provision see Brigford and Stirling, 2000). What we have discussed is an overview of European provision (John Stirling's chapter) and particular examples of representative training, such as European Works Council representatives in Doug Miller's chapter, or the tensions involved in moving towards core labour education programs in South Africa (Linda Cooper). We have also two reports (Tom Nesbit; France Laurendeau and D'Arcy Martin) on educational provision for full-time officers (FTOs), on how FTOs are being equipped to respond to the faster, less certain environment of the globalized economy. FTO training can be considered as an aspect of core labour education that has been overlooked by labour in the past.

Training recruiters could also be classified as representative (and FTO?) training and therefore as another new development within core labour education. In organizing education, the Australian *Organising Works*, the US *Organizing Institute* and the UK *Organising Academy* are important labour education responses to the decline of union membership and to shifting employment patterns (as discussed by Marcus Widenor and Lynn Feekin). The work undertaken in organizing immigrant workers in Los Angeles is a particular example that has been successful in linking union activity to community groups and community-based organizing with labour education playing a key role (as documented by Kent Wong). The *Justice for Janitors* campaigns have been most impressive and have relied on educational support to bolster activity, recruitment and contract negotiation. The region around LA has bucked the trend in the US, providing a leading example of union growth. Some of this educational and organizing work involves existing union representatives and some of it is targeted at new members and would-be union representatives.

New developments in other labour education

As argued in the opening chapter, while *tools, issues* and *labour studies* might describe the majority of labour education, the definitions do not encompass all labour education offerings. Unions are directly involved in several membership education programs, some of which have a "basic skills" or vocational purpose (as illustrated in the chapter by Chris Holland and Geraldine Castleton). The importance of this work for union building has been established in Scandinavia, Britain and Australia and is now being realized in Canada and elsewhere. Other initiatives around union-provided basic literacy courses or vocational training courses can give organized labour a lever to improve the quality and general applicability of such programs in contrast to the often workplace-specific emphasis of many employer sponsored courses. Union negotiated "employee development schemes" such as those at Ford's UK plants are also contributing to broader educational opportunities for union members (Beattie, 1997).

Britain's UNISON Open College, which includes labour education, basic skills, recognition of prior learning and vocational training opportunities for all union members, definitely represents a way forward for labour education (discussed in Forrester's chapter). This program connects with members' immediate needs and in time feeds into strengthening union activity and presence in society. It can also provide critical approaches to current issues, something which is lacking from more homogenized adult education and training. UNISON has recognized the failure of much basic adult education and stepped in with a *Return to Learn* (R2L) program that provides opportunities for workers to become better educated. Further, they have laddered that introductory course up through their Open College to other programs, even to the attainment of full degrees. It takes the "learning society" rhetoric seriously and accesses employer and state funding and claims time-off work for its members. The courses are based on UNISON developed educational material. Its link with the Workers' Educational Association for tutoring of R2L assures an adult education focus, with materials centred on collective understandings. This educational initiative is benefiting the members and the union (Kennedy, 1995).

Fernando Lopes has illustrated how, in Brazil, *Programa Integrar* has come to offer relevant vocational training and educational opportunities for union leaders, employed members, and the unemployed that again work to strengthen the union presence. The program Fernando discusses illustrates how difficult it is to establish union education in a hostile climate but also how ambitious labour education can be in building the union and seeking to change society.

Women and youth

Two important areas that have not been extensively discussed in this volume are labour education for women members and for youth. Many unions and labour organizations worldwide design educational events and schools that reach out specifically to these two sectors.

In Saskatchewan, Canada, an example of labour education for women is the Prairie School for Union Women (PSUW), organized by the Saskatchewan Federation of Labour (SFL) each spring since 1997. The impetus for setting up the school was the same as it is for many women-only educationals – to provide an environment where women feel more comfortable about expressing opinions and are perhaps more likely to participate than at traditional union schools. As one facilitator put it, "Women who are activists in male-dominated unions often find themselves expressing ideas [at the PSUW] they have withheld for years" (Gerlach, 2000). The school offers an intensive four days of learning and sharing experiences in a supportive environment, with the goals of assisting women to develop interpersonal and leadership skills and building solidarity among women workers.

The PSUW is a residential school, taking place at the Echo Valley Conference Centre about an hour's drive from the Regina, the province's capital. For many years in the late 19th and first part of the twentieth century, it was the location of a tuberculosis sanitarium, and some who have attended the PSUW say they have seen the spirits of those who lived and died there. Enrollment for the School is limited to 200, and participation rates over the years have always been very close to that maximum number. In the 2001 PSUW, 180 women, mostly from Saskatchewan and other Prairie Provinces, took part.

The school is planned each year and operated by the SFL and volunteers from within the labour movement. Each workshop has two facilitators, and it is not uncommon for the facilitators to have been participants themselves a year or two previously. The workshops and other events take place over a four-day period composed of two two-day tracks. Workshops cover a wide range of equity, labour and social justice topics, and there is also a focus on health and well-being. Participants, for example, can choose Taking it to the Streets (a primer on the art of civil disobedience), What's There to Laugh About (using humour to alleviate stressful situations), Shop-Floor Militancy (organizing and building solidarity in the workplace), or learn how to communicate more assertively in Finding Our Voices.

The PSUW organizers always plan activities and services aimed at nurturing the body and spirit as well as the mind. Outside of workshop hours participants can hike, attend a yoga class, get a massage or shiatsu treatment, or treat themselves to a manicure. In order to ensure access to all union women, on-site daycare is provided for children aged 12 and under. The fees for attending the PSUW are covered by the participant's union and include course materials, accommodation, and meals.

Another event organized by the Saskatchewan Federation of Labour is the SFL Summer Camp for Kids, for young people aged 13 to 16. This week-long residential camp introduces the teen-aged sons and daughters of SFL-affiliated union members to trade unionism and social justice issues in the morning and offers recreational activities that emphasize cooperation as well as fun in the afternoons and evenings. The educational component of the camp includes sessions on health and safety issues in the workplace; harassment, sexism, racism, and other "isms;" and the annual negotiation of the collective agreement between counsellors and campers that sets the camp rules for the week. The long-tem goal of the camp is, of course, to bring new activists into the trade union movement. Apparently the camp is successful in this goal, as according to a four-time counsellor, it's not "uncommon" to see former campers at conventions and protests or walking a picket line (Banks, 2000).

In another initiative for youth under the age of 26, the Canadian Labour Congress (CLC) has joined with provincial federations of labour in offering a summer, three-week program called Solidarity Works! This hands-on training initiative focuses on activist skills development and labour education.

The pilot of this project took place in the summer of 1999 in Toronto and was a partnership between the CLC and the Ontario Federation of Labour. From August 3 to 20, participants spent one week in a course of labour education and then worked with unions and community-based organizations in projects that linked the training they'd received in the first week to practical and real situations and campaigns. That first summer, participants helped out in ongoing initiatives such as an anti-sweatshop campaign, a survey to identify young Canadian women's issues and how they might be addressed, a discussion forum for young women that was located in a Toronto coffee shop, a community legal services clinic, and a large-scale Labour Day youth event.

The three-week pilot was a great success, and participants continued working on issues and campaigns with labour and community groups throughout the year. Based on that success, Alberta launched a Solidarity Works! for the following summer. By the summer of 2001, Saskatchewan had joined in, and it is likely that two additional provinces will also launch Solidarity Works! in the summer of 2002 (Canadian Labour Congress, 2001).

Reflections on the future of labour education in a globalized economy

The importance of the UNISON initiative, outlined above, for the future of labour education cannot be overstated. Similarly the negotiated (as opposed to state) paid educational leave (PEL) programs in Canada offer another important example of membership education, one focused on developing critical political understandings. The origins of this program can be found in the UAW initiatives in the US but the CAW has led the way in creating a membership education program independent of employer influence, and now CUPW has followed with something similar. Other unions in other countries need to examine the possibilities of this approach. The main features of this program include a negotiated, employer-paid levy to a union-controlled trust. The union uses the fund to pay for lost wages and expenses of its members who attend the core four-week residential PEL course. The weeks in the core course are separated and have themes such as history, sociology, political economy and social and political change. Experienced union activists who have undertaken "discussion leader training" tutor the courses. By targeting these courses at members (not representatives) the unions seek to engage their members' imaginations and draw them into greater union understandings and activity. The core four-week program has been supplemented by other courses also funded from the levy (Spencer, 1994).

Labour education, broadly defined, has also begun to challenge issues of workplace learning, new management techniques and globalization discussed above. Keith Forrester reports on developments on the workplace learning/union interface in the UK. Some of the evidence flowing from union involvement in workplace learning is contradictory and there has been a growing recognition by those involved of the problematic nature of union-workplace learning initiatives. In another paper, Keith Forrester has cautioned that the "brave new world of 'empowerment,' 'autonomy,' satisfaction and fulfilment within those 'new workplaces'" can just as likely lead to "new mechanisms of oppression and managerial control;" if that is the case, there is the danger that "the brave new world of pedagogics in relation to 'work and learning' will become a part of the new forms of oppression and control in the workplace" (1999, p. 188). Nonetheless, as Keith argues, unions are trying to seize the initiative and establish "learning representatives" as union representatives responsible to the local union organization. Although research circles (workers conducting their own research into workplace or sector problems) have been around for some time, it is clear from the chapter by Gunilla Härnsten and Lars Holmstrand that this approach has a bright future in strengthening union activity within the union as well as externally. It represents an important alternative for union members wishing to conduct independent "workplace learning" projects, and the method supports participatory democracy within unions and in society.

Courses on new global management techniques have developed with colourful titles such as *Union Judo* – a metaphor for using the "weight" and "momentum" of the employer to union advantage (Martin, 1995). Nor have unions ignored free trade and globalization itself. These topics are by their nature difficult for unions that are single-country based, but additional emphasis has been given to international union activity in the last 10 years, and not just on courses for union representatives from works councils of transnational companies discussed by Doug Miller. Unions have increased their presence on international bodies discussing environmental, conservation, and sustainable development issues, and these initiatives have an educational component (Gereluk & Royer, 2001; Spencer, 1995). Unions have responded to calls for international workers' solidarity with some courses not only dedicated to creating a greater understanding of the issues but also involving study visits and exchanges. In other examples union educators have built units on solidarity work into basic steward courses and into membership courses such as the CAW PEL program (Luckhardt, 1999).

As Jeffery Taylor documents (and John Stirling noted), unions have also responded to educational challenges posed by widespread computer use and the Internet with the development of a solidarity network (SoliNet) in Canada in the early 1990s, and a continuing investigation of the uses of on-line education for union members in the new century. Jeffery Taylor argues for e-learning to be a tool that unions use to supplement and support other forms of union education and organization. An obvious use for labour on-line learning is to build education across national boundaries.

The movement of production to less economically developed countries by some transnational corporations does provide a threat to unionism, but the response of international union federations and some individual unions (sometimes aided by NGOs) to seek "framework agreements" may result in new opportunities for unionization in those countries. These agreements reached with corporation head offices push them to only do business with suppliers who recognize workers' rights and independent unions. It is difficult to predict whether or not these measures will be successful in developing unions in countries such as Indonesia, The Philippines, Thailand and China, but once organized, these unions begin to develop their own labour education programs, and union education initiatives are already underway (see Rita Kwok Hoi Yee's chapter for a discussion of some of the issues and methods involved). Will this and the other international and solidarity initiatives discussed above be enough? Perhaps not on their own, but the existence of these labour education initiatives means the future is more open than might be predicted otherwise.

Many of the initiatives discussed in this book have elements of both accommodation and resistance to current globalization trends. Some courses and programs can be seen as proactive, others as adaptive, while much of labour education remains reactive. Overall, however, unions remain an important and positive social organization for working people. It is the absence of strong, independent unions that remains a problem for workers in the majority of free-trade zones, and labour educators understand that. But beyond these immediate concerns unions do have to wrestle with the question of what it is they want to achieve. Are they simply striving to represent members within the new global order, or should they, as Mike Newman urges, strive to become key players in civil society? If they choose the latter, there are implications for labour education; the focus of labour education would shift (but never retreat) from representative training – core labour education – towards courses and programs stressing education for community development, strategic involvement and social justice.

Labour education has always been "social:" core labour education is provided for representatives rather than for individuals, and it has always had a social purpose – that of improving the conditions of workers at work and in society. As illustrated in this collection, labour education today is more diverse and ambitious than it has ever been in serving the needs of both representatives and members as they face the challenges of the twenty-first century.

REFERENCES

- Banks, C. (2000). Kids camp. *Briarpatch* 29(8), 24-25.
- Beattie, A. (1997). *Working people and lifelong learning: A study of the impact of an employee development scheme.* Leicester, UK: NIACE.
- Bridgford, J. & Stirling, J. (Eds.). (2000). *Trade union education in Europe.* Brussels: European Trade Union College.
- Canadian Labour Congress (2001). http//www.clc-ctc.ca/youth/works.html
- Gereluk, W. (2001). *Labour education in Canada today.* Athabasca, Alberta: Athabasca University.

- Gereluk, W. & Royer, L. (2001). Workplace research and education for sustainable development. In *2ⁿᵈⁱ international conference on researching work and learning*, Calgary: University of Calgary. 536-543.

- Gerlach, L. (2000). Sisterhood in the classroom. *Briarpatch* 29(8), 20-22.

- Forrester, K. (1999). Work related learning and the struggle for subjectivity. In *Researching work and learning: A first international conference.* Leeds: University of Leeds. 188-197.

- Kennedy, H. (1995). *Return to learn: UNISON's fresh approach to trade union education.* London: UNISON.

- Luckhardt, K. (1999). International working class solidarity: From cold war back to the class war. *Briarpatch* 28(8). 17-32.

- Martin, D. (1995). *Thinking union: Activism and education in Canada's labour movement.* Toronto: Between the Lines.

- Spencer, B. (1994). Educating union Canada. *Canadian Journal for the Study of Adult Education, 8*(2). 45-64. (Revised version in D. Poonwassie and A. Poonwassie (Eds.), 2001, *Fundamentals of adult education.* Toronto: Thompson Educational Publishing, pp.214-231).

- Spencer, B. (1995). Old and new social movements as learning sites: Greening labour unions and unionizing the greens. *Adult Education Quarterly* 46(1). 31-41.

- Wray, D. (2001). What price partnership? Paper presented at *Work Employment and Society* conference, 11-13 September, University of Nottingham.

Index

basic skills/education 20-21, 32, 134, 143-44, 171
  workplace literacy 22, 89-99

civil society 18, 64, 127-126, 160-168, 176

computers 14, 32, 50, 114-15, 123-24, 125, 127, 129, 143, 149-157, 175

community/community development 14, 24, 54, 62, 70-78, 80, 82, 89, 92, 95, 102, 108, 112, 115-116, 126-127, 152, 163-168, 171, 173-174, 176

curriculum 20, 21, 28, 32, 66, 92, 104, 106, 108, 122, 126-27, 134

facilitators, labour educators as 41, 43, 108, 155, 173

globalization 14, 23, 31, 36, 47, 50, 57, 58, 94, 100, 115, 120, 174-76

human resource management 18, 140-141, 147, 170

human resources 14, 169

immigrant workers 20, 70-78, 171

Justice for Janitors 70, 74, 76-77, 78, 171

labour education programs:
  Athabasca University Labour Studies 19, 150, 152
  CAW PEL program 19, 54, 174, 175
  Harvard Trade Union Program 18, 52, 114
  Labour College of Canada 18, 54, 112-13, 149
  TUTA (new TUTA) 18, 93, 101, 106, 107, 162
  UNISON Open College 21, 23, 145-46, 171-72, 174, 177

labour/union educators 14, 20, 40, 46, 48, 61, 78, 82, 112-13, 149, 150-154, 157, 163-168, 169-176
  facilitators 41, 43, 108, 155, 173
  tutors 20, 32, 170, 172, 174

labour movement 21, 37-38, 43-46, 50-52, 55, 68, 70-78, 81, 82, 93, 99-100, 102, 105-110, 113-119, 145, 149-154, 173

learning/teaching methods 20, 25, 33, 39, 40, 85, 117, 122, 125-126, 135, 157, 176

non-governmental organizations (NGO) 120, 126, 175

Organising Academy 21, 100, 142, 171

Organizing Institute 73, 100-111, 171

Organising Works 100-111, 171

pedagogy 26, 33, 85, 100, 135

political action 93, 113, 121-122, 124, 126, 127

unions:
  business unionism 19, 47
  campaign/ing 17, 19, 31, 65, 70, 71, 73, 77, 102-110, 142, 151, 154, 164, 174
  full-time officer 17, 21, 50-60, 112-119, 171
  organizing model 19, 31, 59, 106, 107, 164
  organizers 44, 45, 47, 50, 70-78, 100-111, 133, 173
  representatives 17, 19, 22-23, 26, 29-32, 34-35, 38, 43-44, 55, 89, 93-94, 96, 118-19, 129-136, 143-146, 162, 170-171, 174-176
  shop steward 17, 19, 42, 45, 54, 145, 170